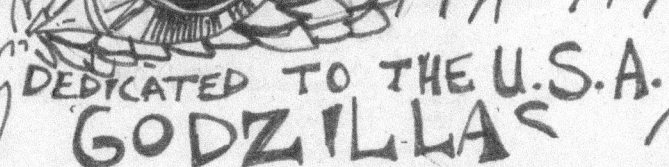

TIAMATZILLA KING OF THE DRAGONS IS WITH EVERYONE ALL THE TIME

DEDICATED TO THE U.S.A.
GODZILLAS

When I was a child in the 80's and Dinosaurs went through a dramatic makeover as science progressed changing their appearance from tail draggers to holding their tails high. The idea was as devastating as changing Brontosaurus's name to Apatosaurus. I was enraged but Godzilla never let me down with his massive mighty tail dragging on the ground and smashing everything he missed with his fist feet and fire. In 1998 a new Godzilla emerged when we had been expecting the father of Dragons and we received the mother (before Lord Queen Daenerys Targaryen of course). It was the Dinosaur evolution of the 1980's all over again only this time with Godzilla. I was mad as King Einon and turned into an abominable monster destroying my soul as I turned against her as Marduk betrayed Tiamat. I cannot ask mother Godzilla to forgive me for my sins for defying her is unforgiveable. I see now she was a true Godzilla. Iguanas are the closest living relative to Godzilla. The face, spikes and plates... offer them some fruit and they will stand right up like the King of the Monsters. Godzilla is a Tyrannosaurs with Iguanodon arms and three large rows of twisted jagged spiked bladed Stegosaurs plates. Where Tristar went wrong was killing off the mother. If she would have been invincible more like in the cartoon I would have been super stoked and looked past any design flaws. The only design flaw was imposing Dinosaur evolution on a tail dragging Godzilla. Godzilla also represents the Tyrannosaurs that should have defeated Kong. For all of those rooting for the Dinosaurs, it makes it hard to support Kong. The battle between Dragon and monkey is captured in the inspiration for Tiamatzilla vs the Kaiju Kongs giving the world a Lizard God to triumph the gorilla monkey king. Dragon Lizard Lord loves Godzilla. Now in the future we have two Godzillas battling for the crown. Where we at Dragon Lizard Lord give Godzilla 2000 and 2014 our full support as the best Godzillas ever with the best ending, it seems to be Shin would make a better Orga than Godzilla. He is not a true Godzilla like the Legendary, Classic, Heisei or even Tristar Lizards. This is much more like Destroyah and has an Otachi jaw. Otachi was the closest they had to a Dragon in Pacific Rim and would have made a great Wyvern if its bottom jaw did not spit in half when he opened his mouth ruining the whole Dragon aura it had going. So Toho changed Shin's jaw to open in this manor, combined with arms like Scary Movie's Chris Elliot and a body ripping off the look of the Nemesis monsters from Project Mango, Hyperion and so forth with eyes that are best described as fish like that never shut and a body full of humans. Shin also turns into a statue when powered down acting like a robot and is bloodied by the military when they call in the "big guns." I'm sorry but try as I might these changes to Godzilla go far beyond "Dinosaur Evolution." In the USA our new Godzilla can take any fire that Shin has and deal it back 10 fold. Praise Legendary. Our Godzilla can take it but Shin would turn to stone and shatter into zombies that Legendary Godzilla would nuclear pulse to oblivion. Our first Godzilla should have created a Dragon's rule of Godzillas being the new rulers of the Earth with eggs not evolving into an army of people but growing into massive Godzillas to take the throne of the world. It would have been wiser to get Roland Emmerich and Dean Devlin back to finish what they started than to unleash Shin on us. Godzilla is the symbolic protector of earth, piss him off and face his wrath. The Legendary Godzilla IS A FORCE OF NATURE. Shin obviously is not. Toho is coming around good with the deal God incarnate being the meaning for the name Godzilla. Mad props to Toho on supporting Godzilla as God. His new fire and powers were very impressive. Tiamat is the first God, a Dragon from the first writing of man. I present to you now a truly omnipotent God Lizard, Tiamatzilla Dragon King of the North Sea! -Omar M. Sayyah
p.s. Enjoy my bonus Tiamat Goddess Dragon mother comic at the end of the maze! Good journey Dracolytes!

KING LOUEY
NOW BEHOLD HIS OMNIPOTENT MAGESTY
AND HENGH FORTH I DUBB THEE...
TIAMATZILLA!!!
KING OF THE NORTH SEA
MY LIZARD, MY FATHER, MY BROTHER, MY SON, MY GOD ALL IN ONE.. AND WE WILL RULE AS DRAGONS FOREVER — omar m sayyah

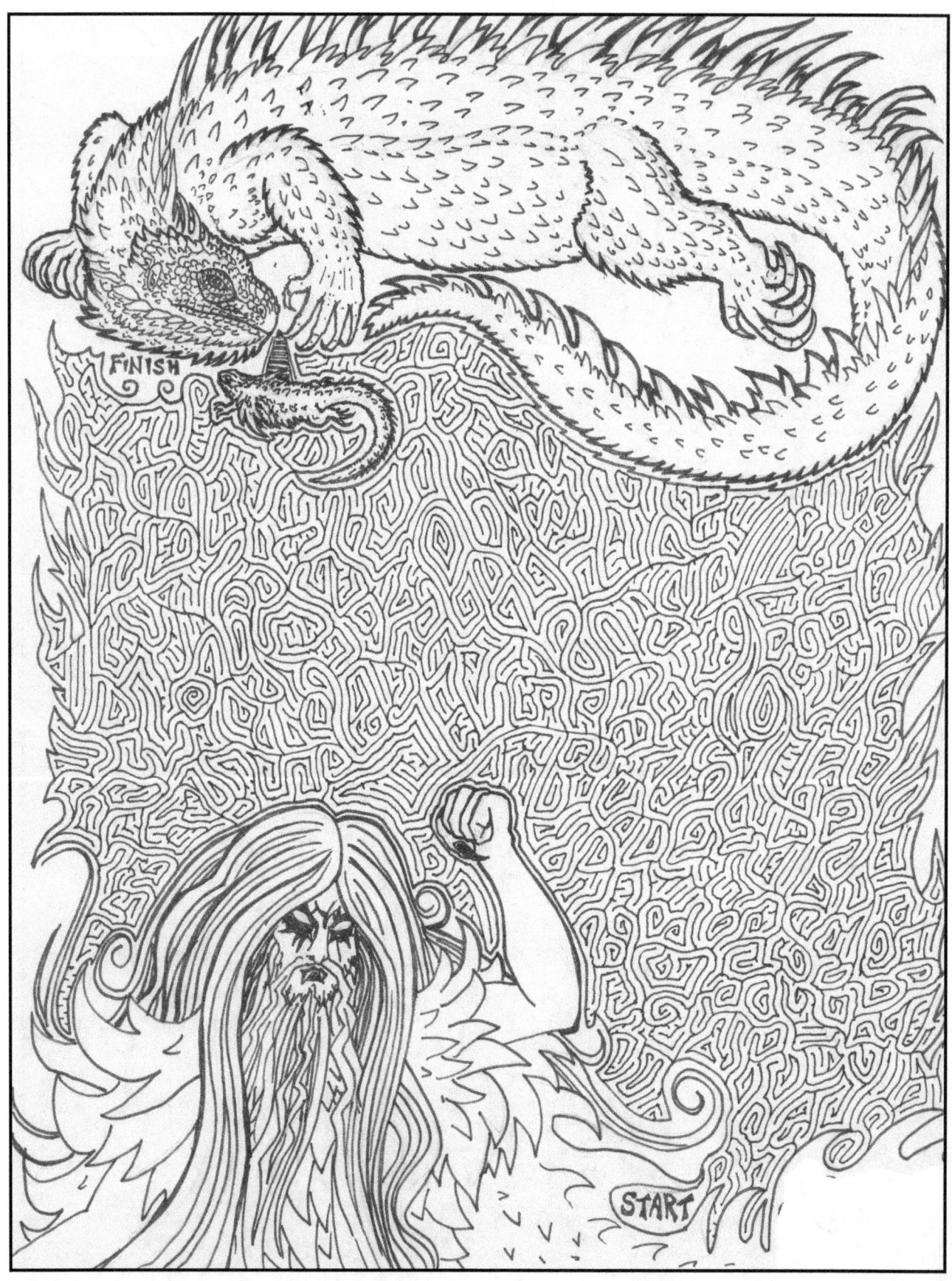

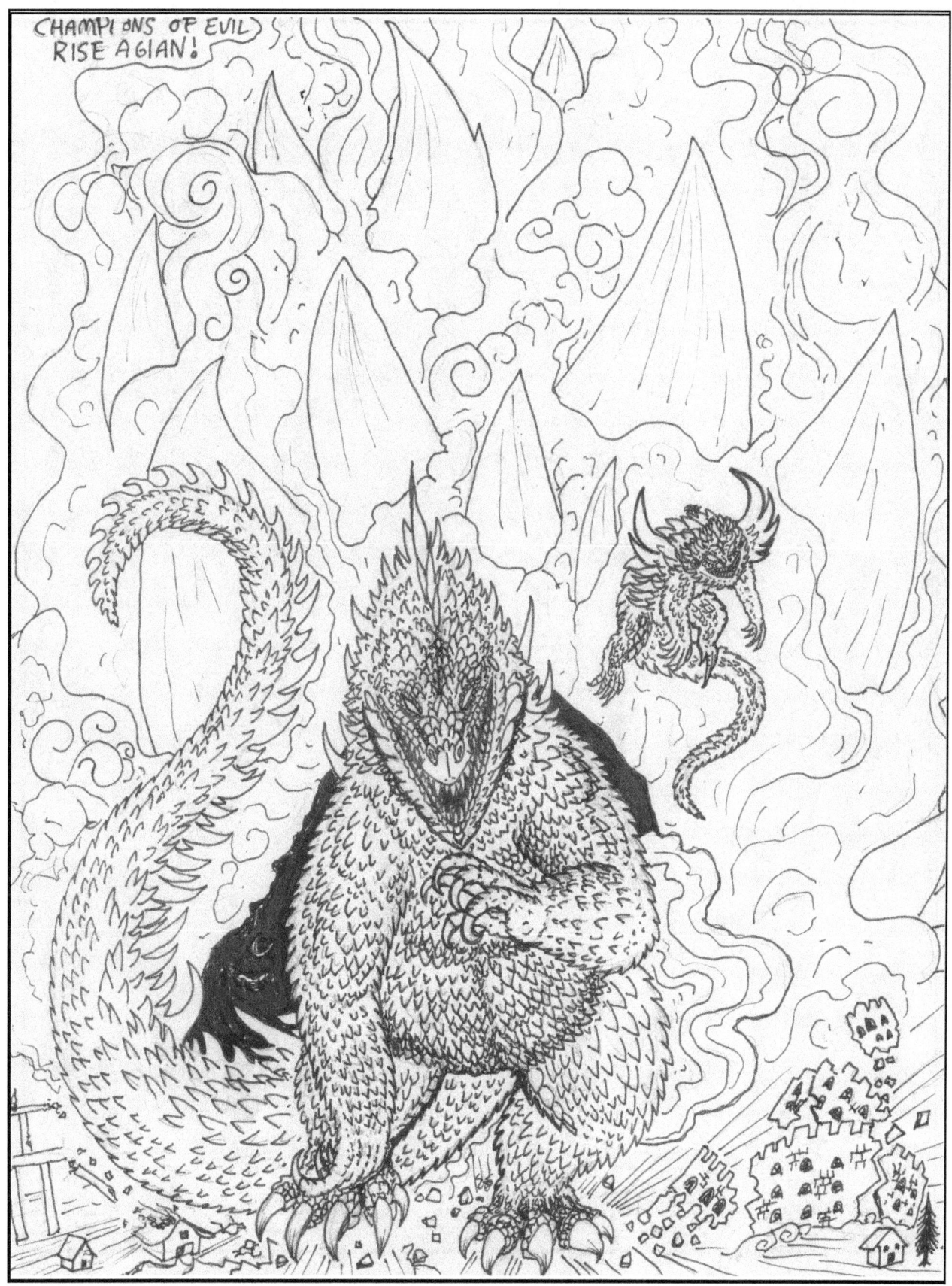

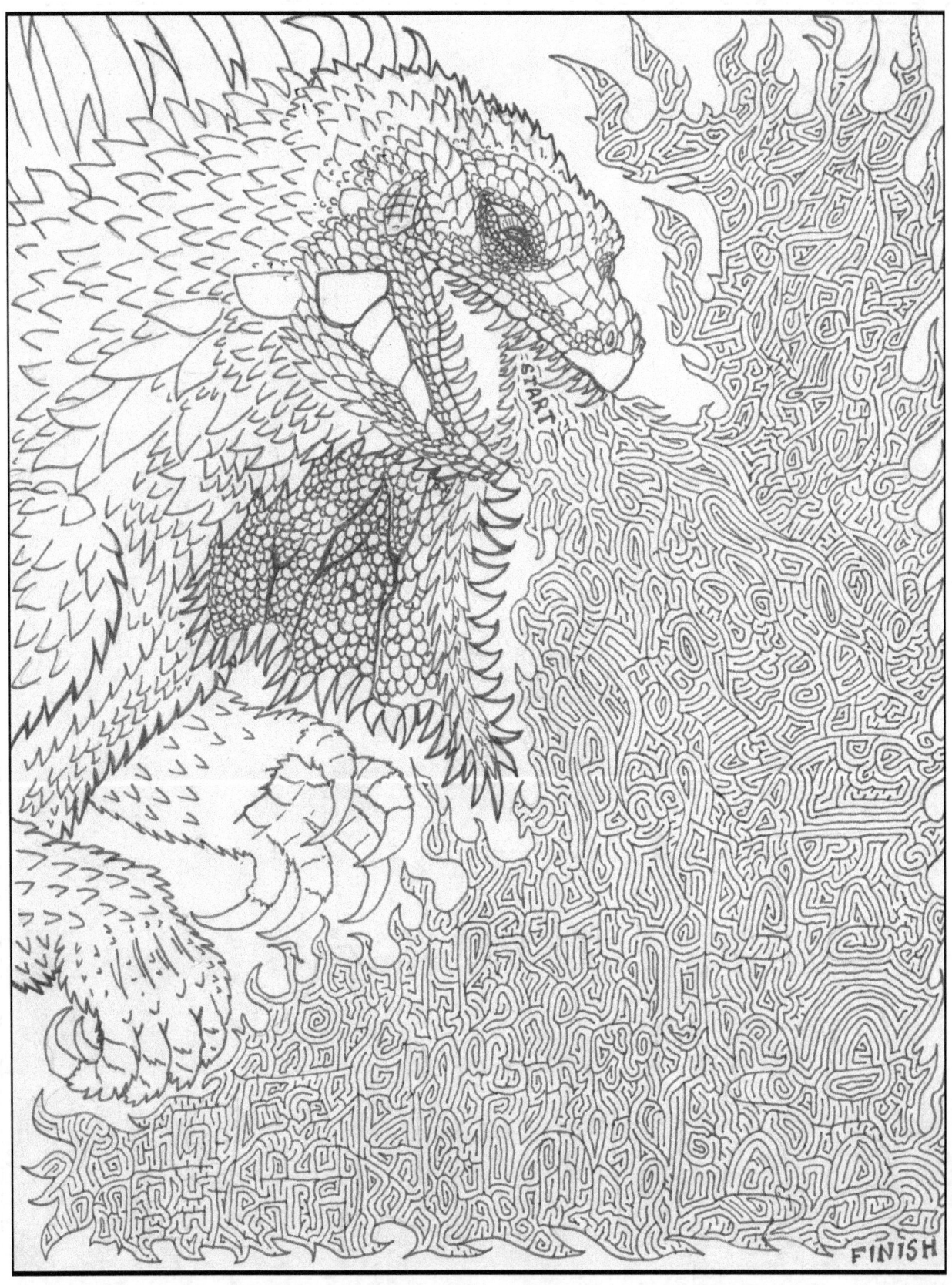

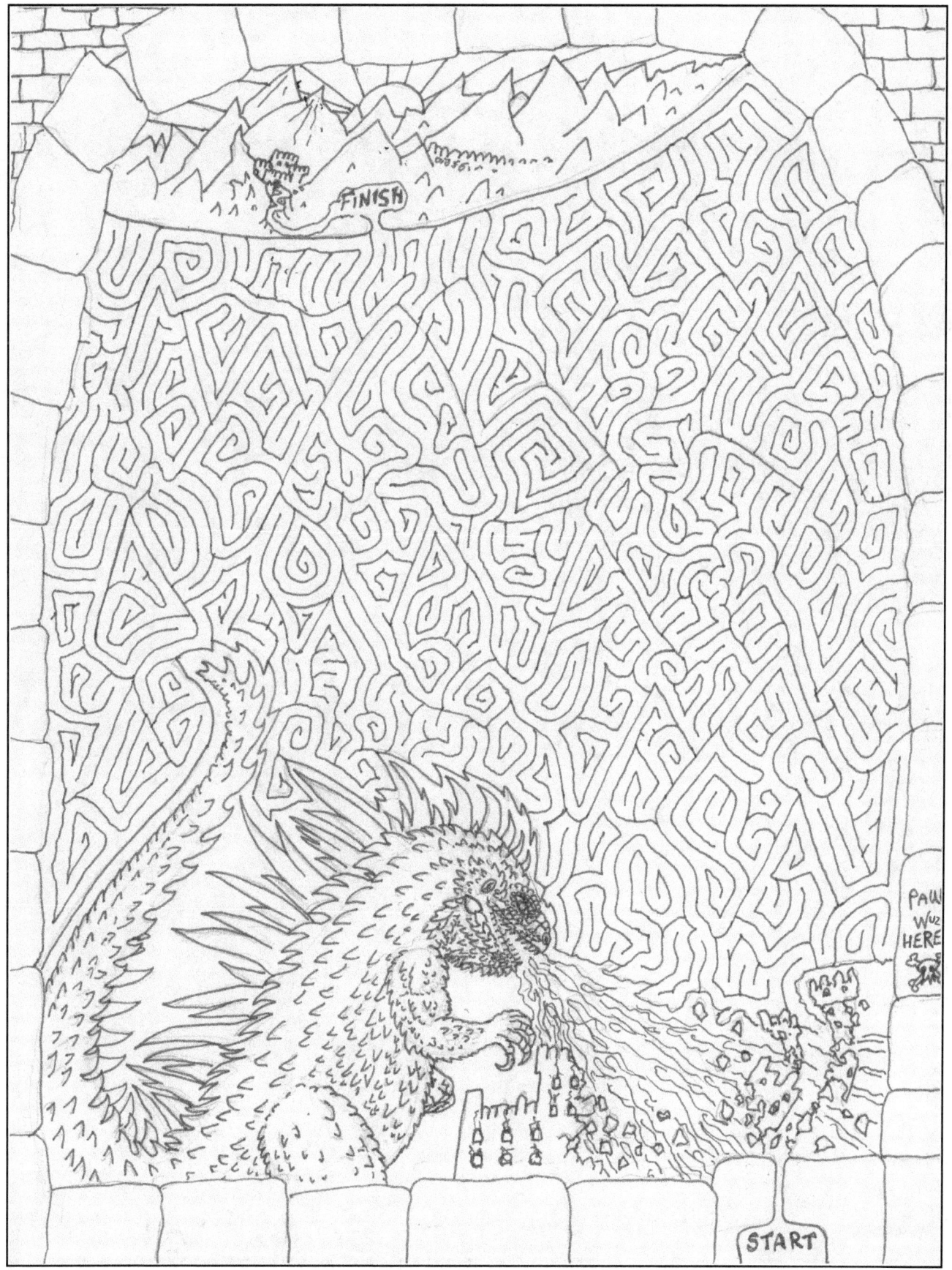

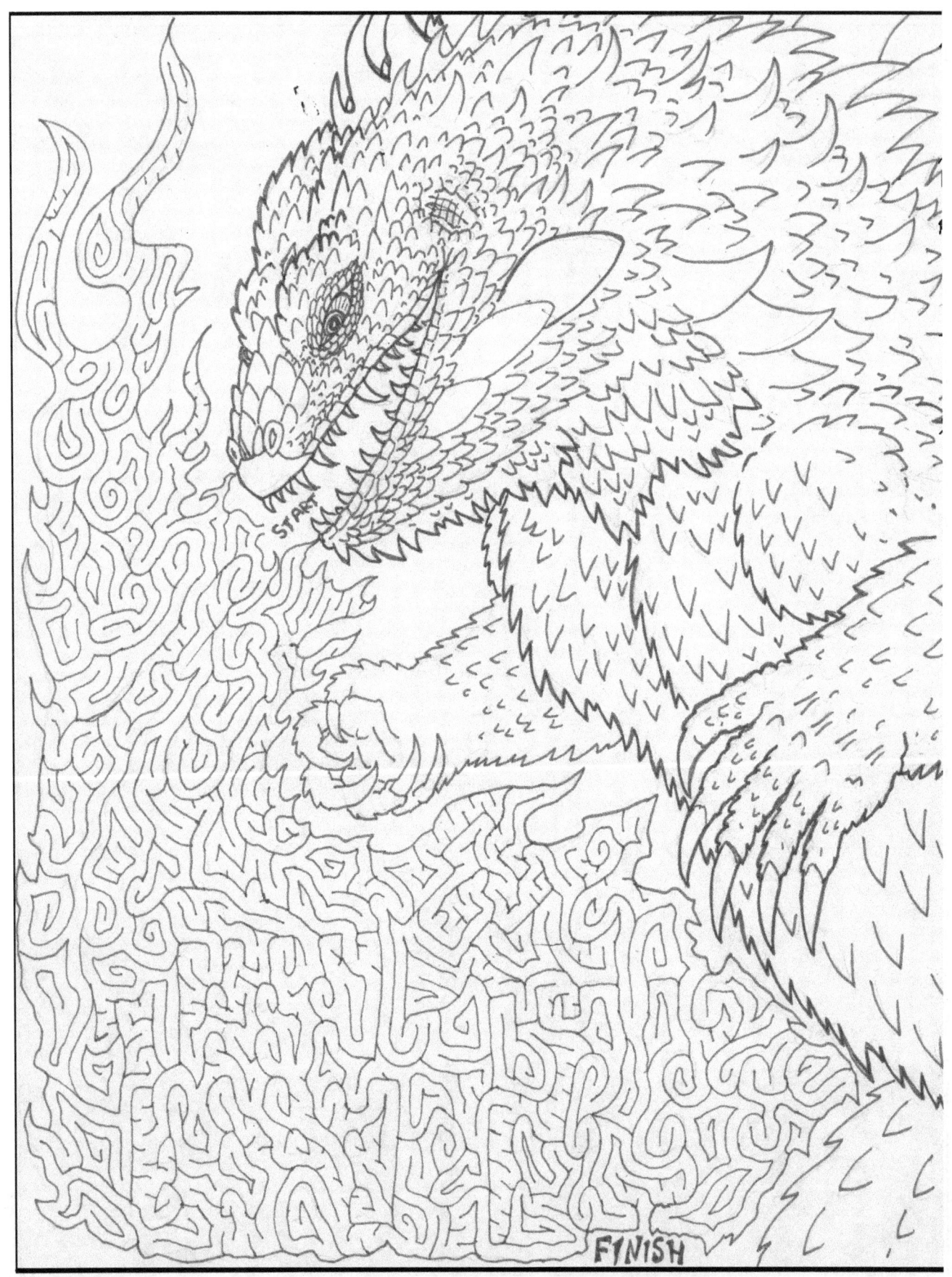

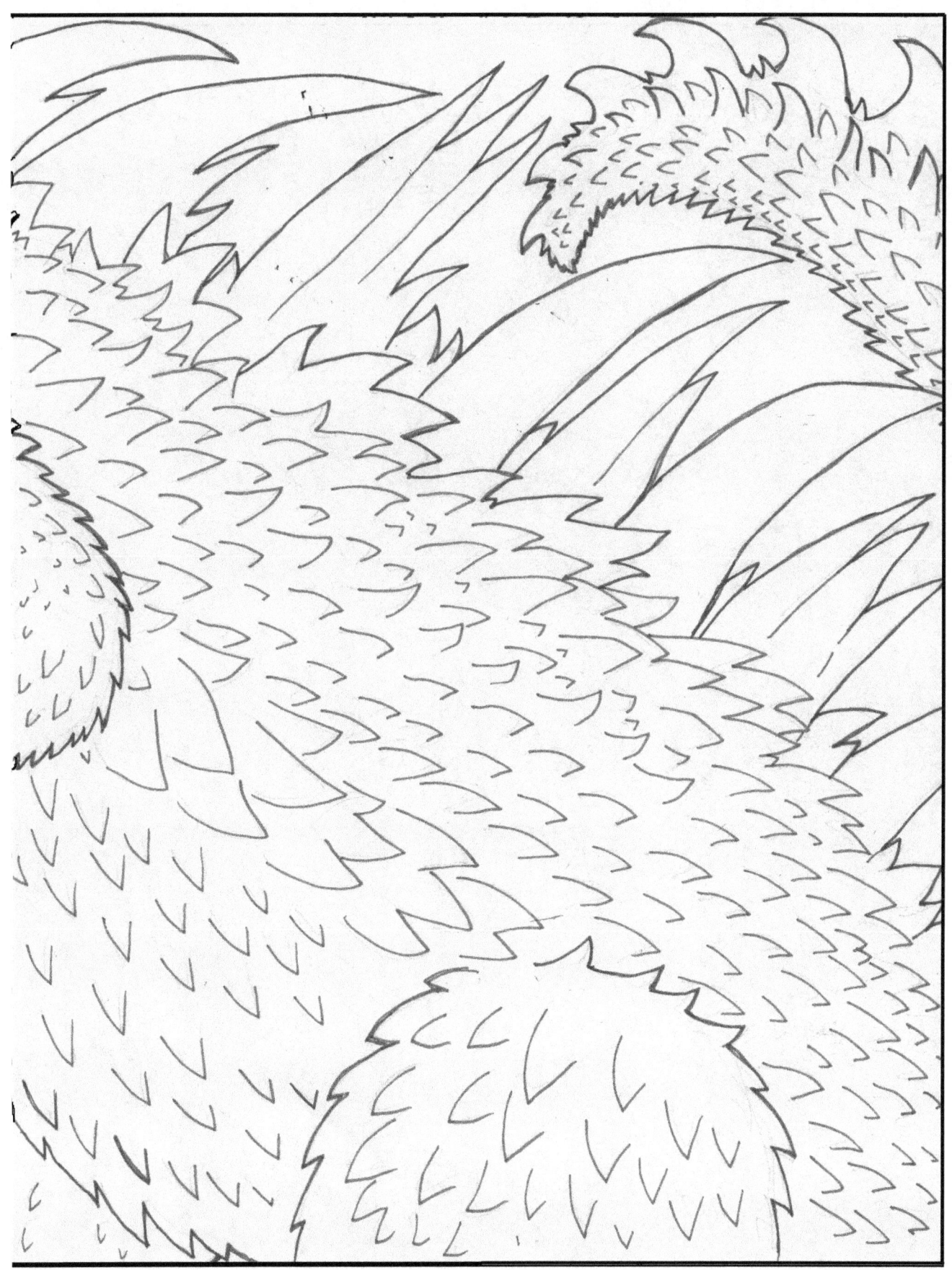

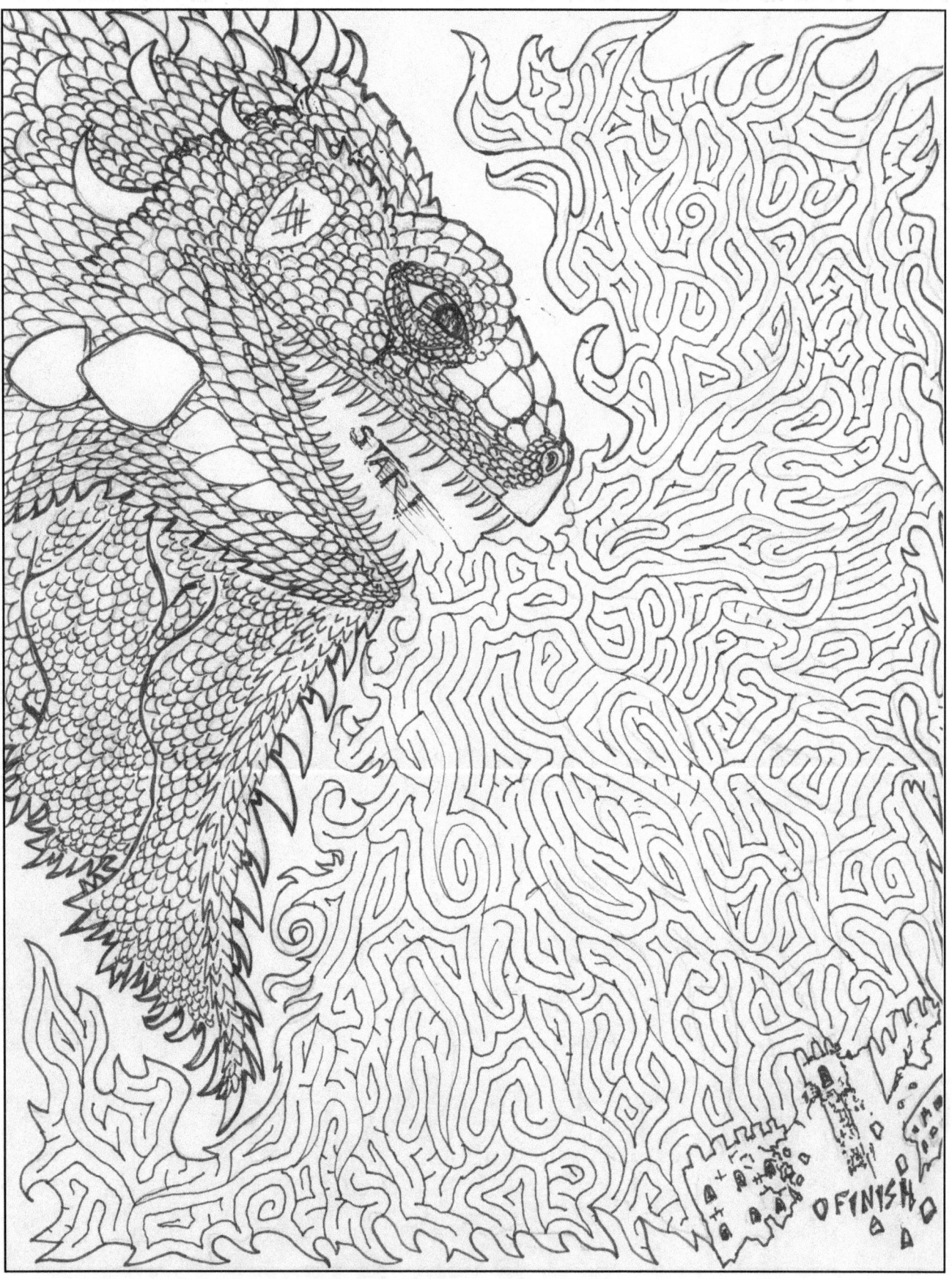

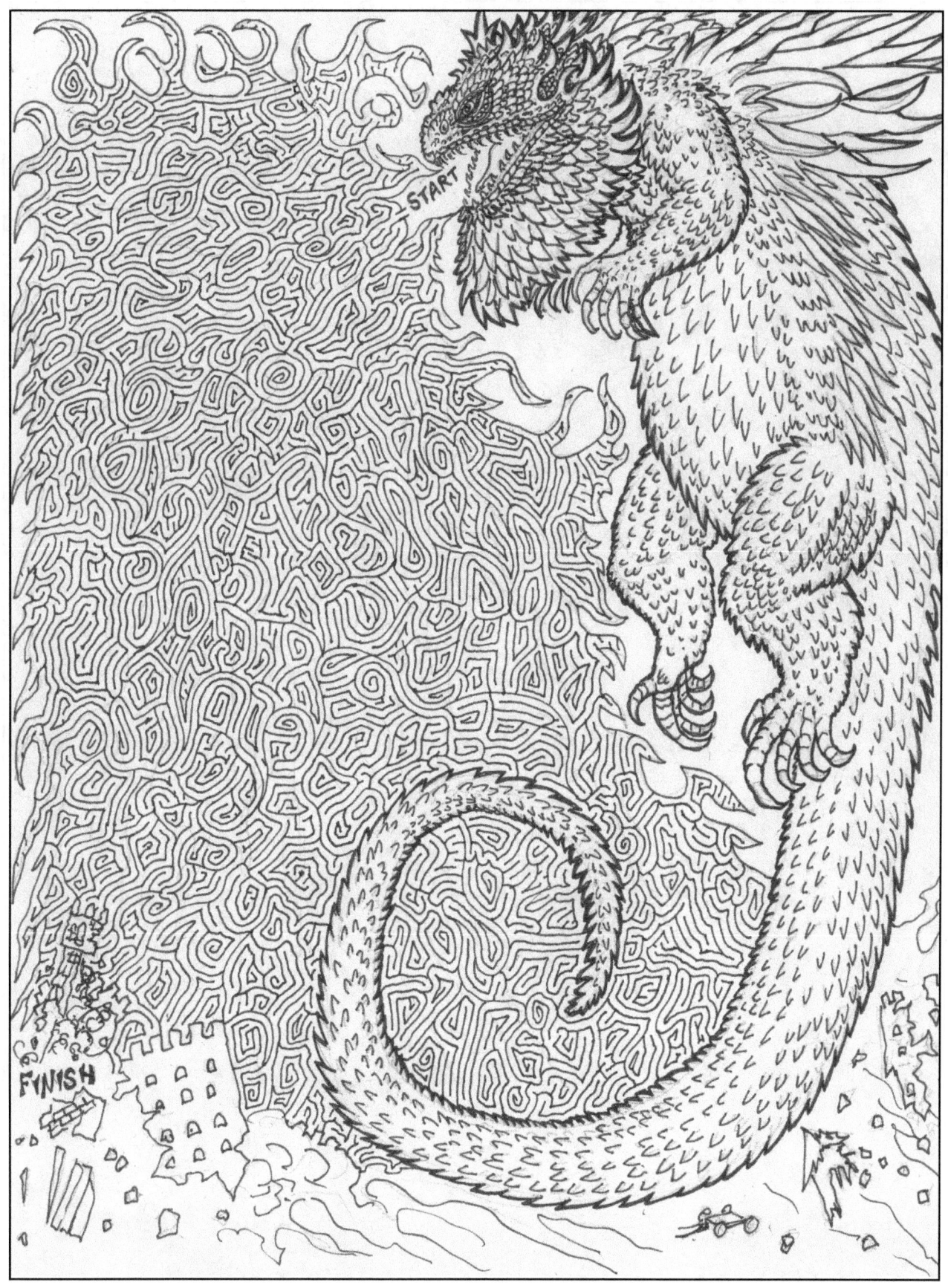

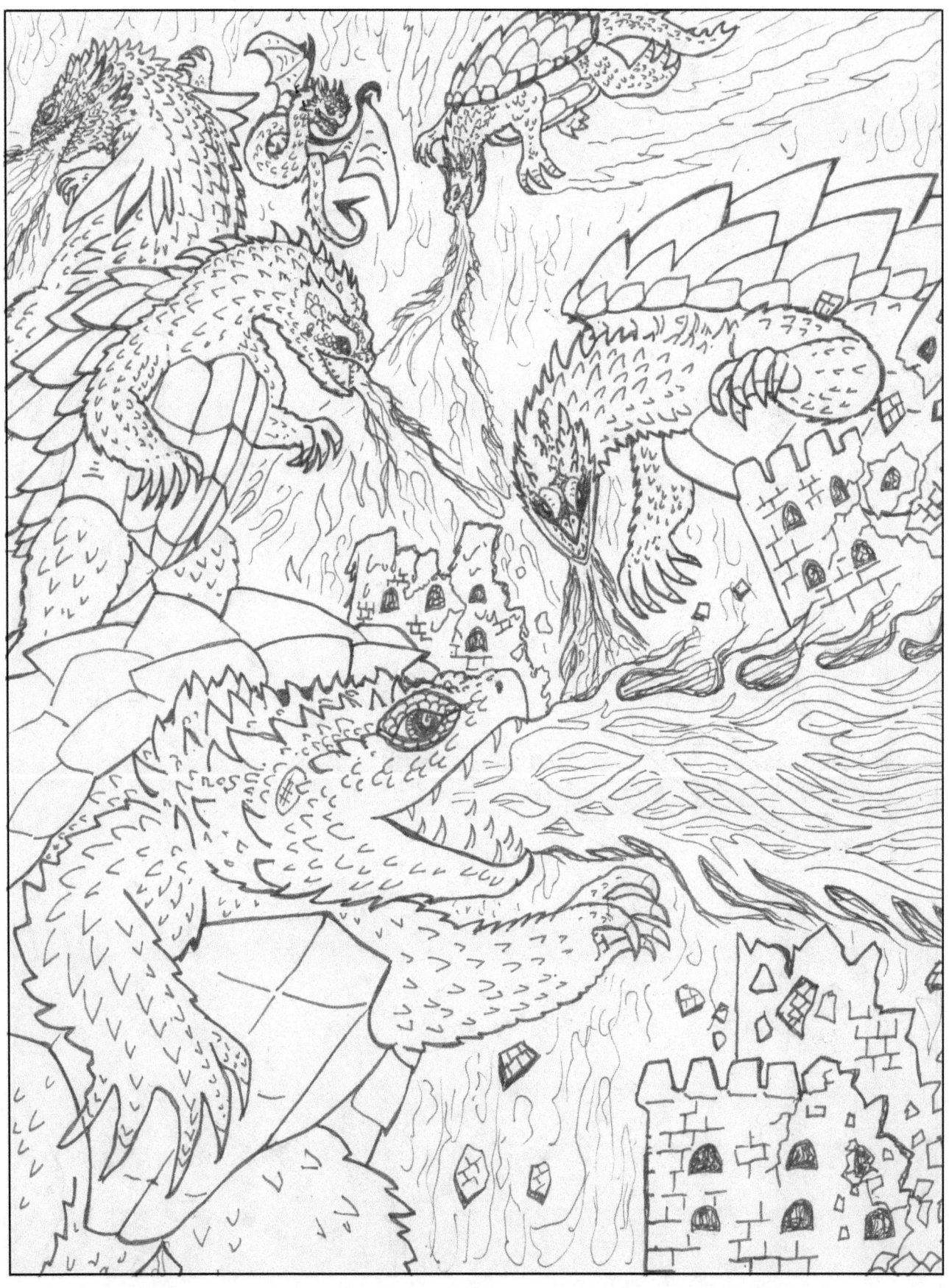

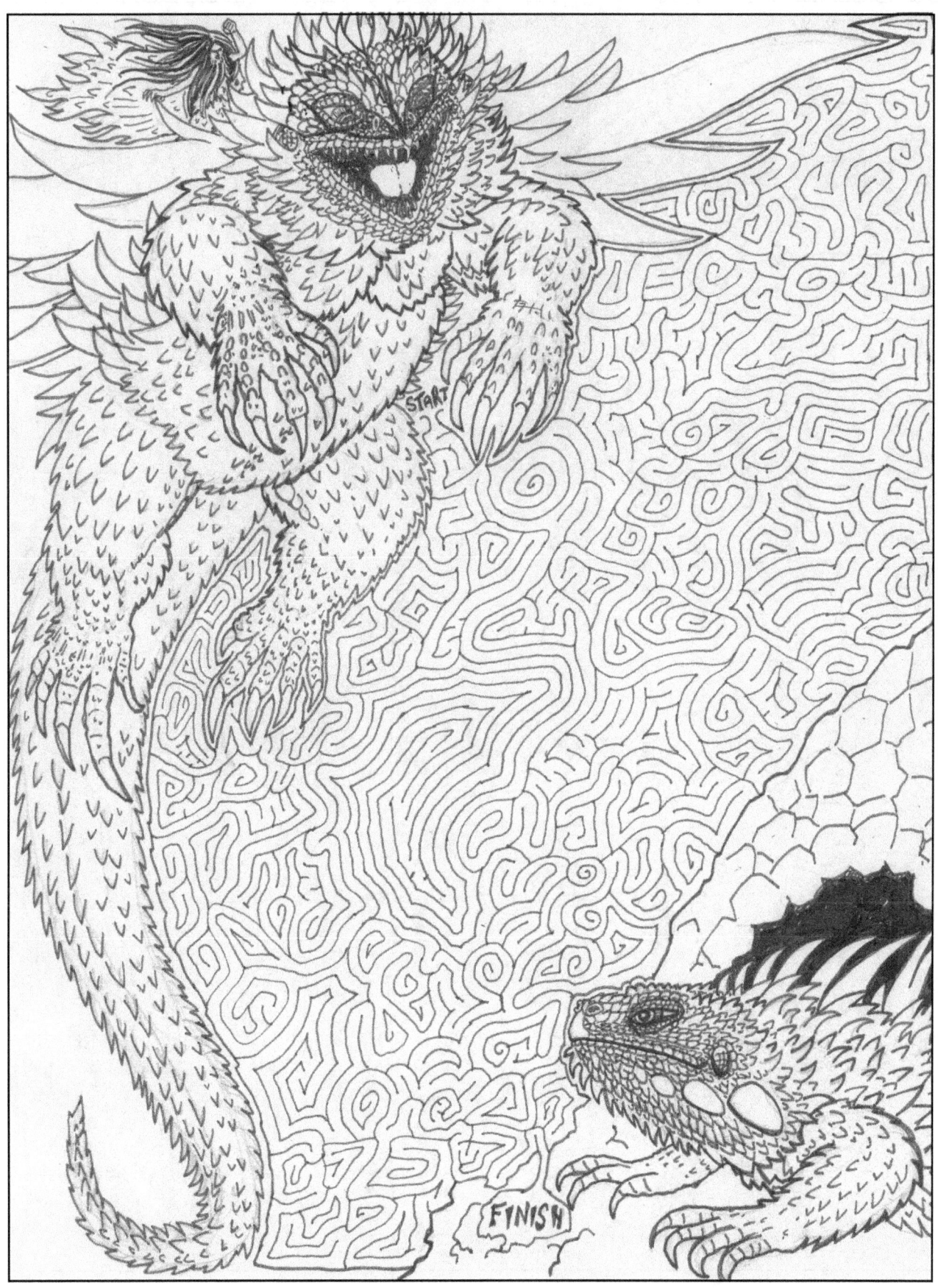

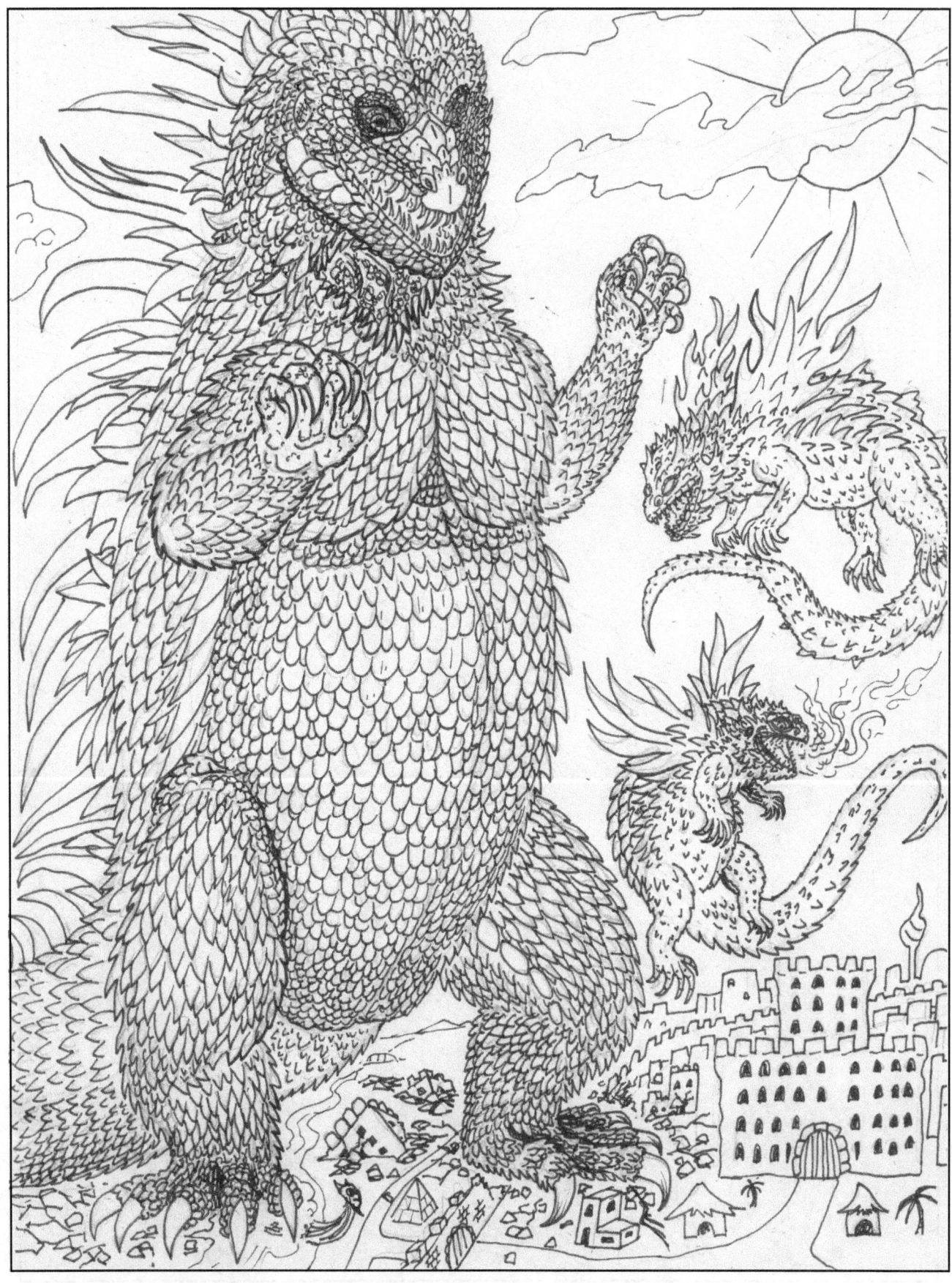

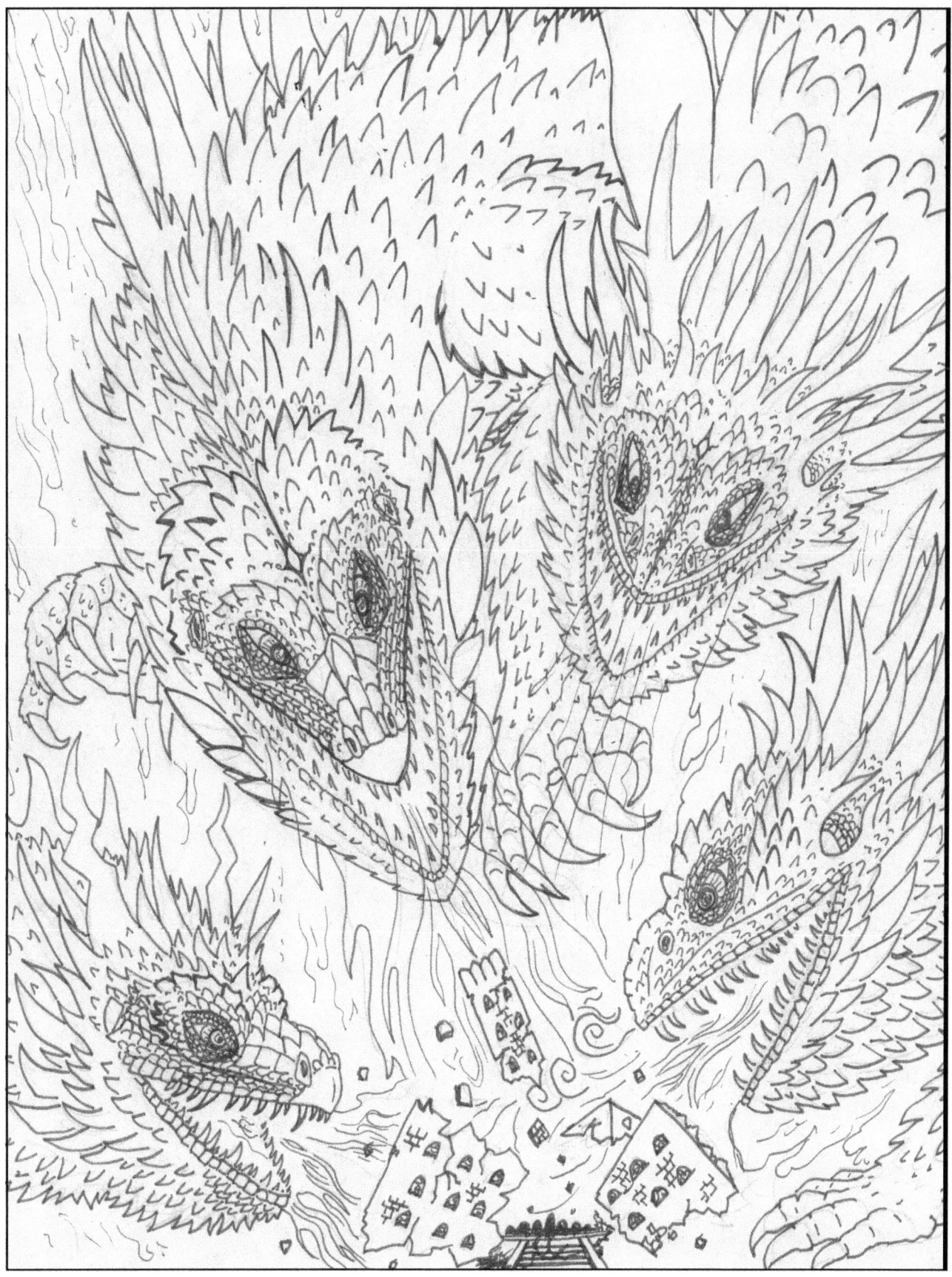

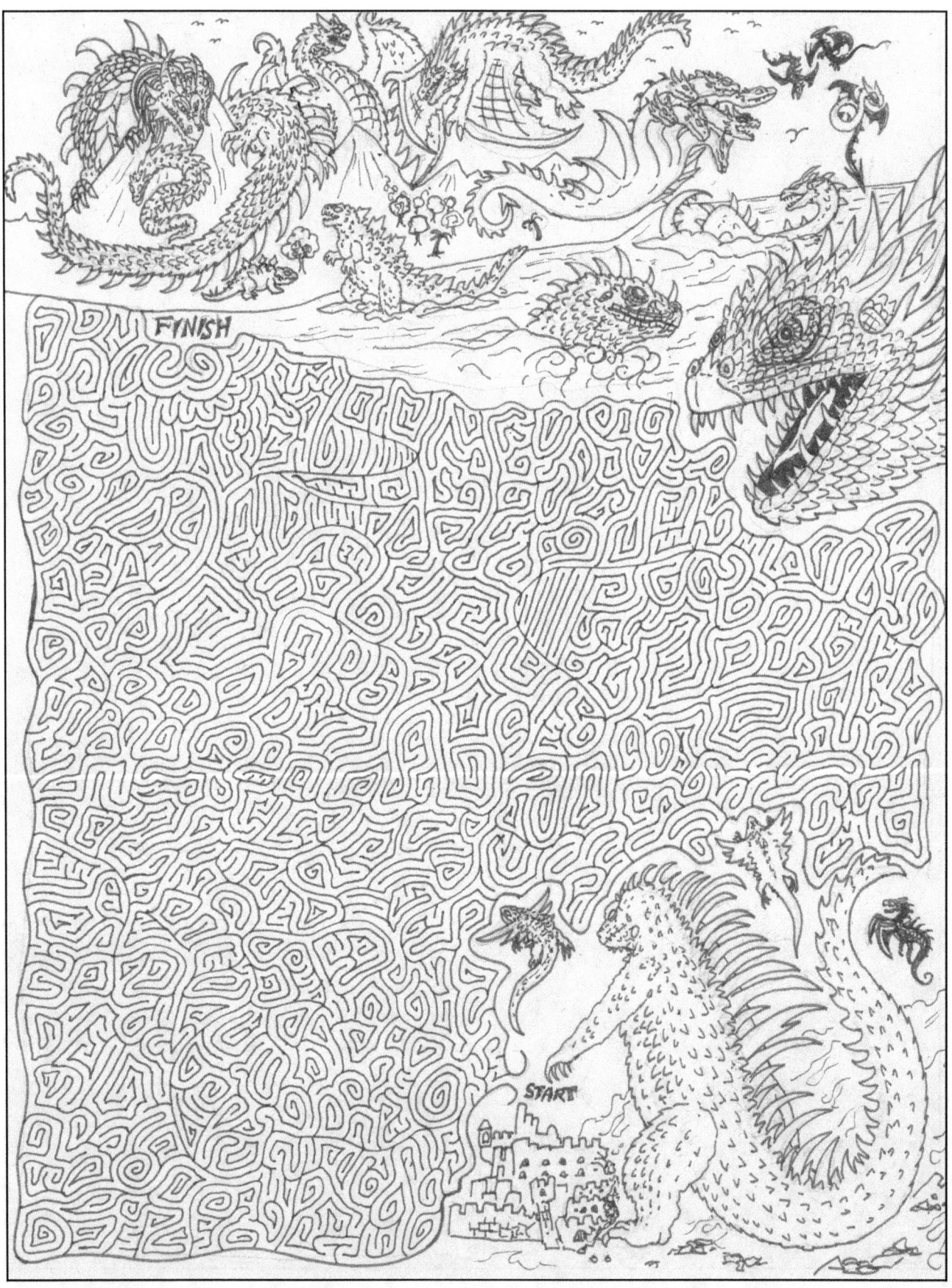

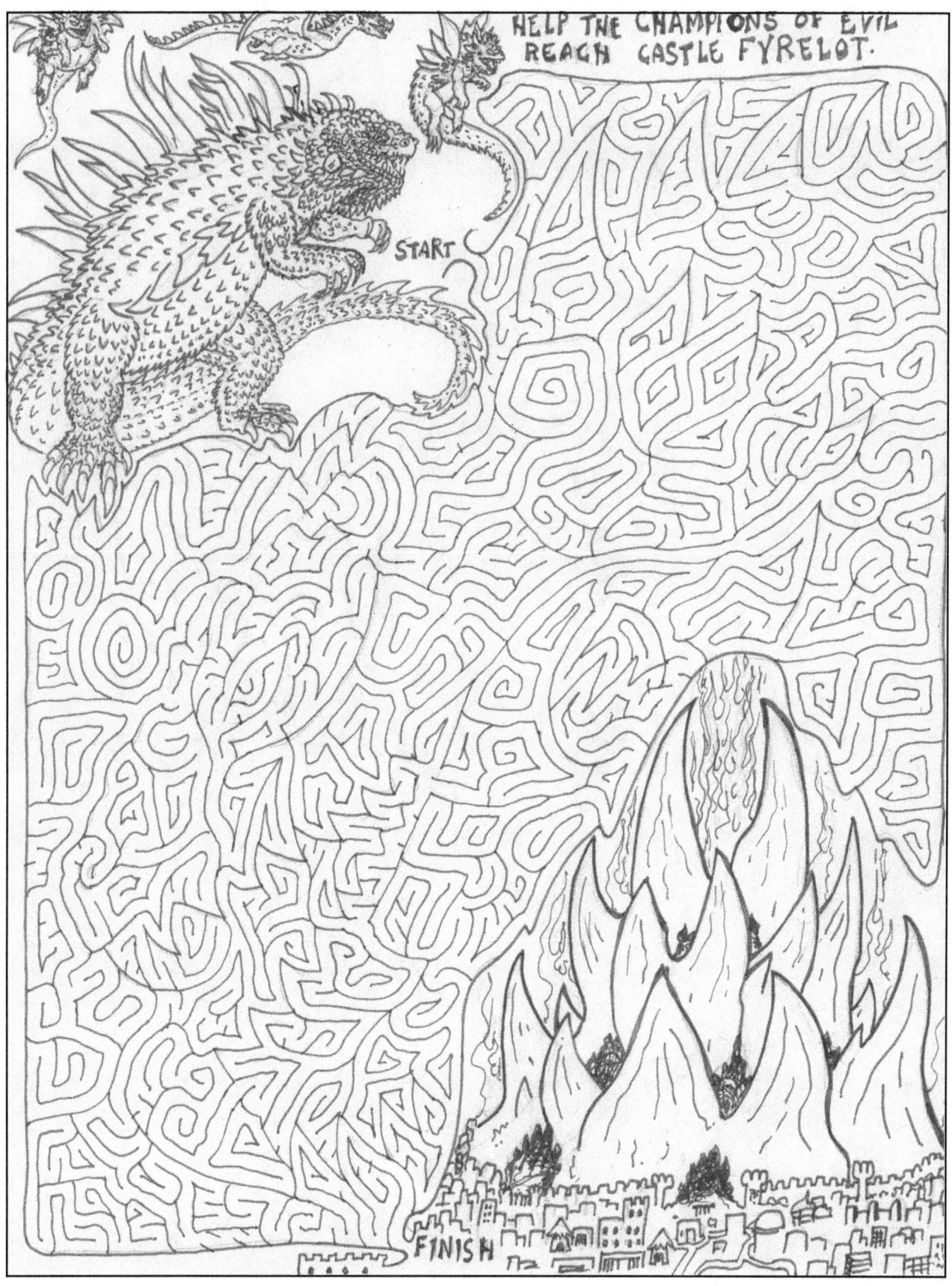

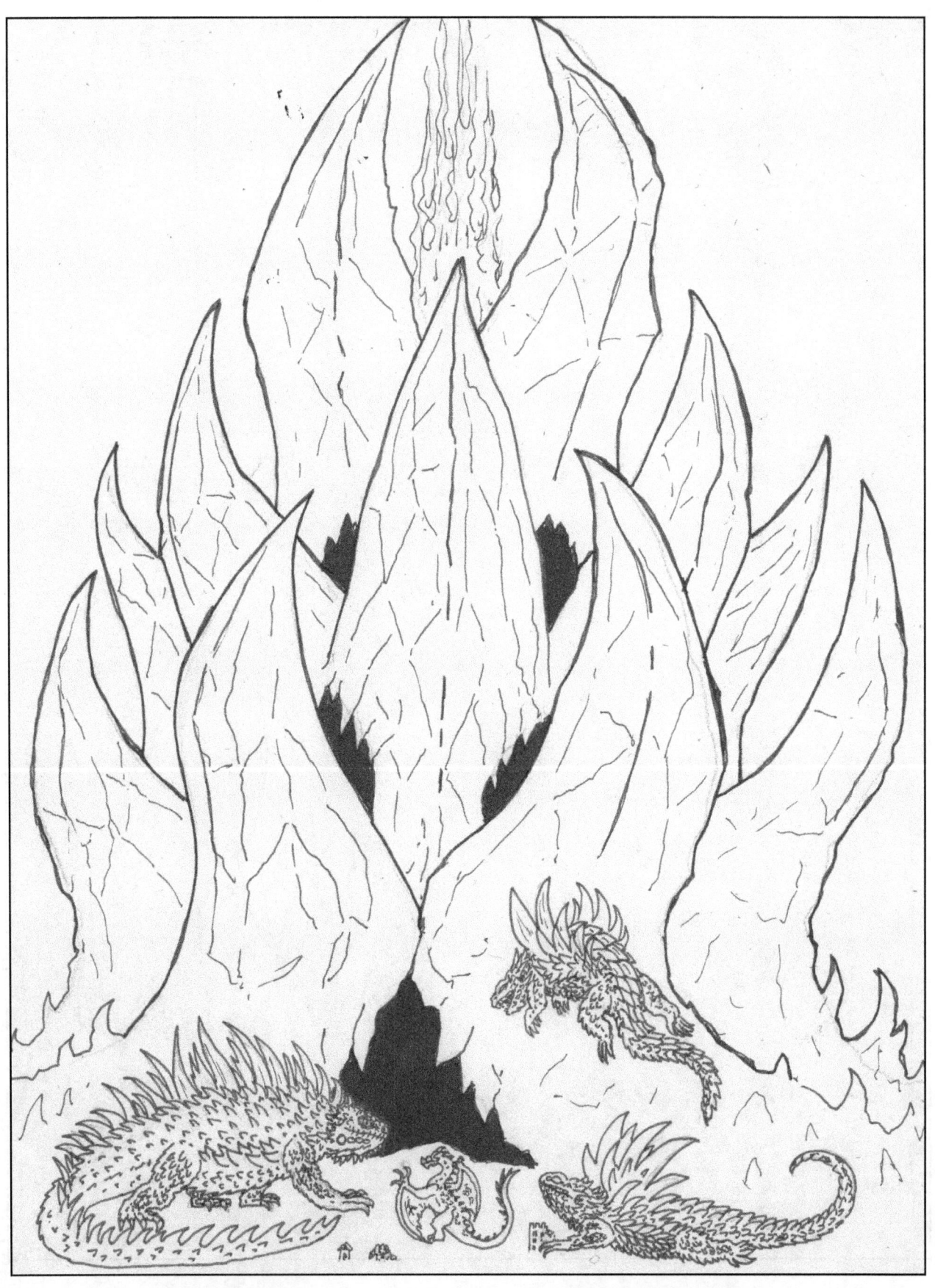

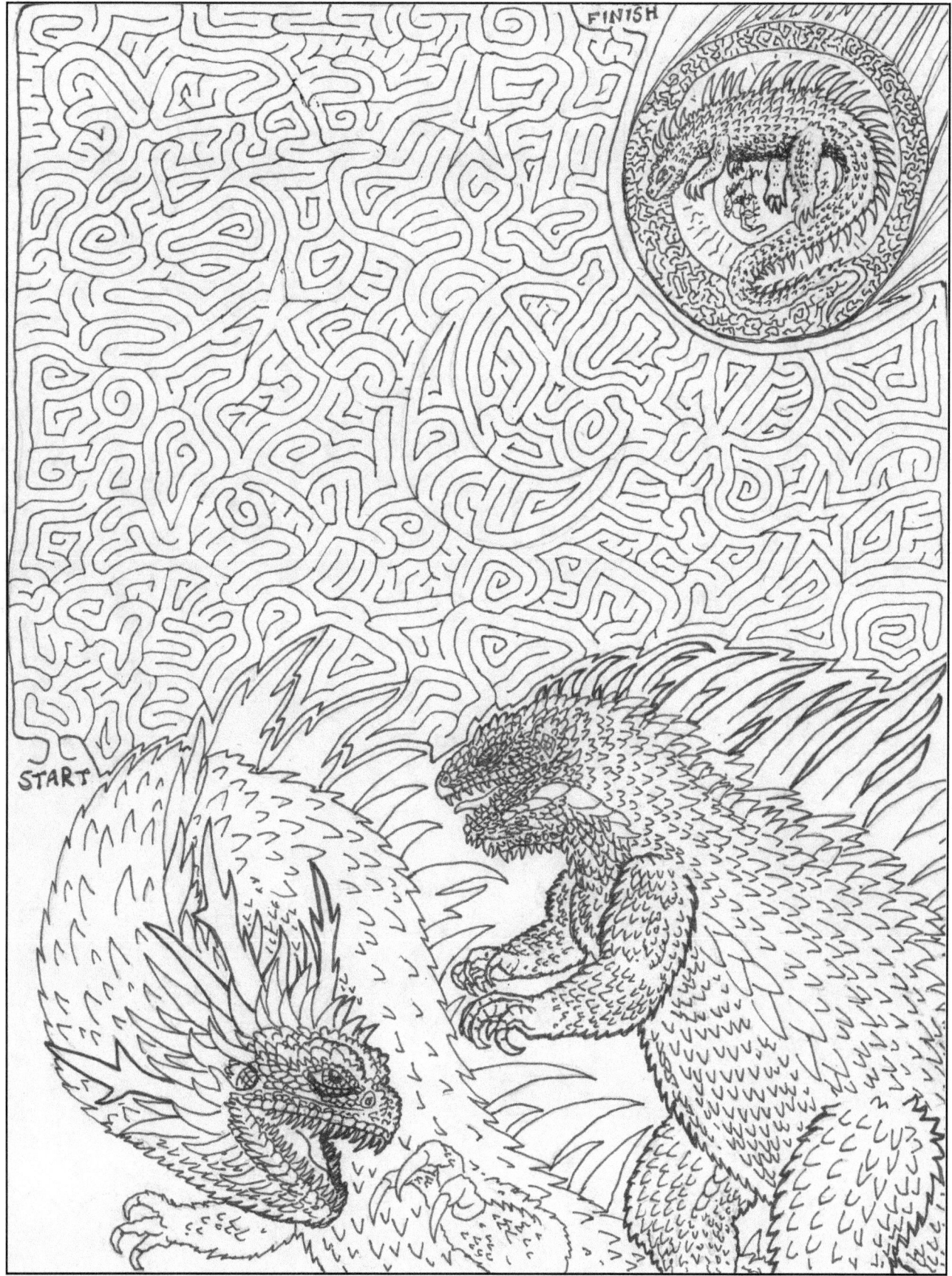

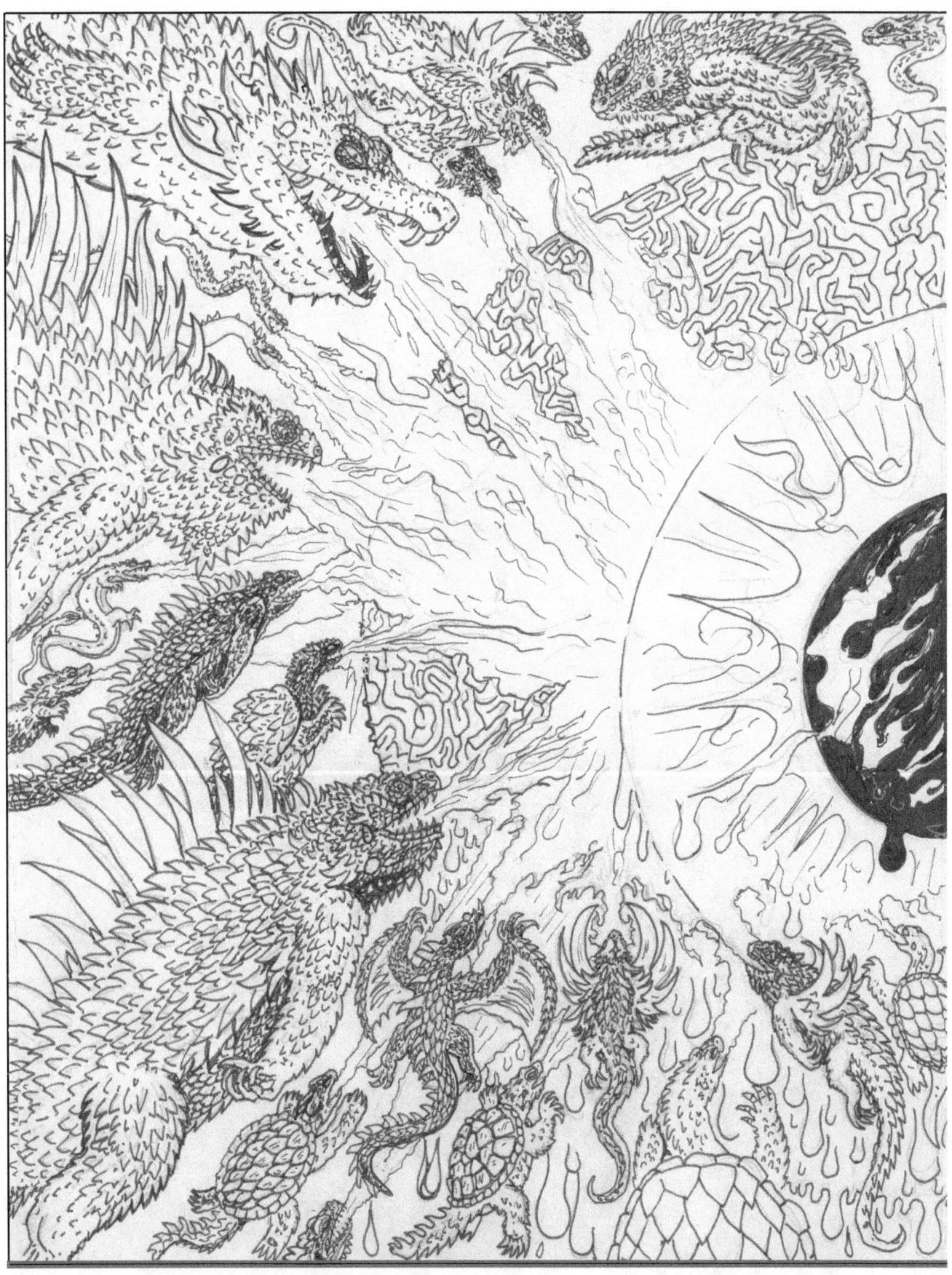

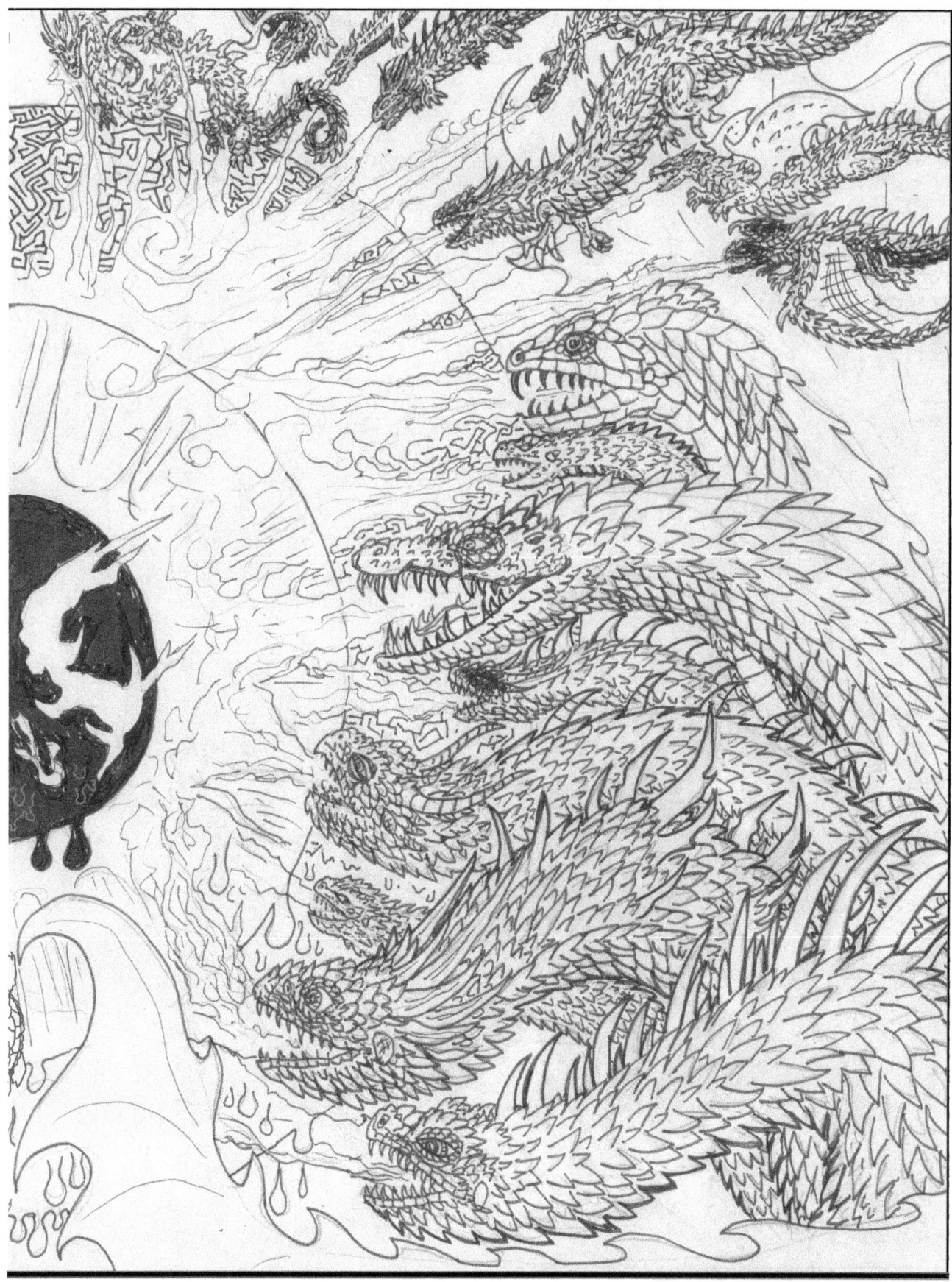

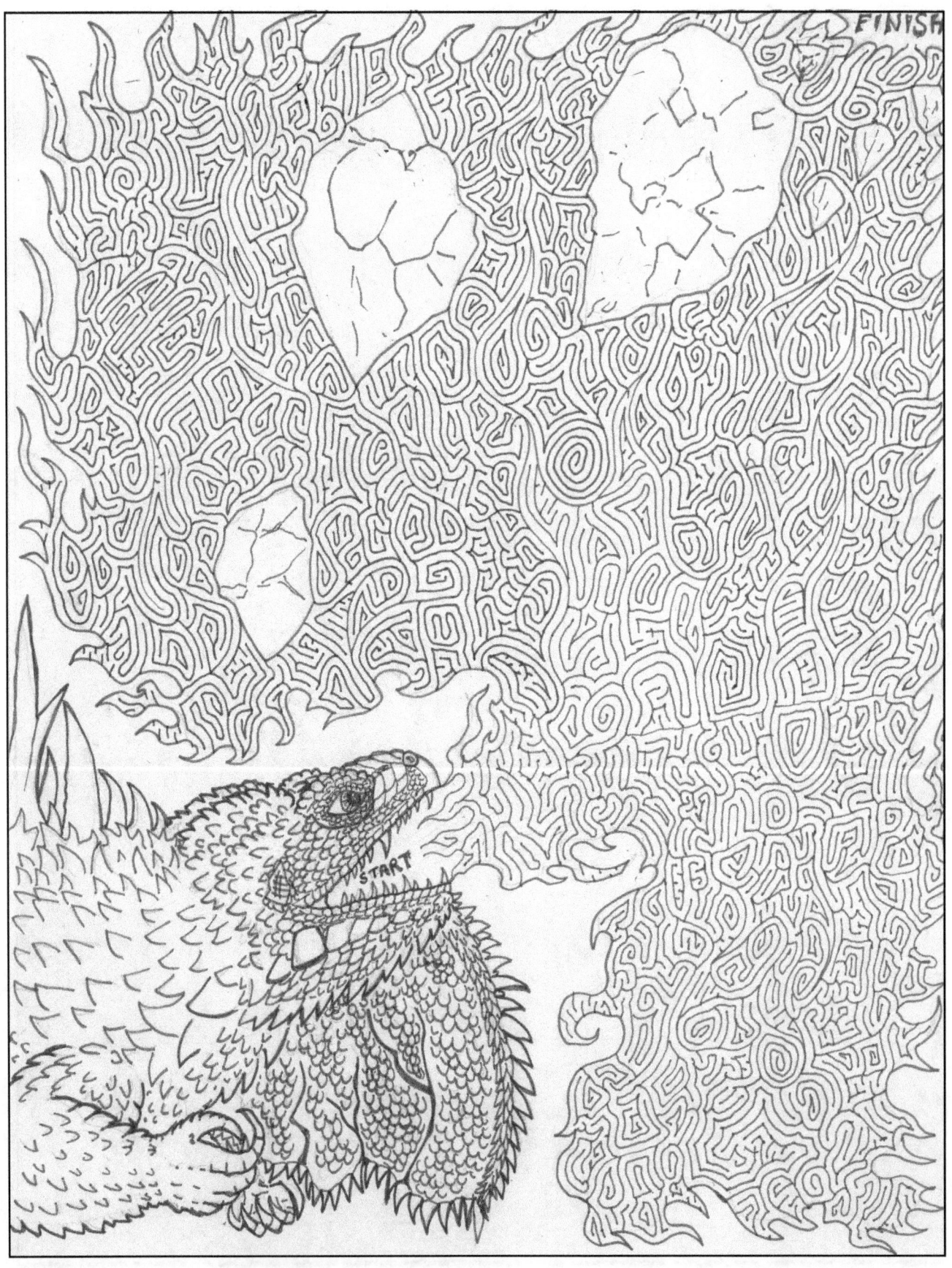

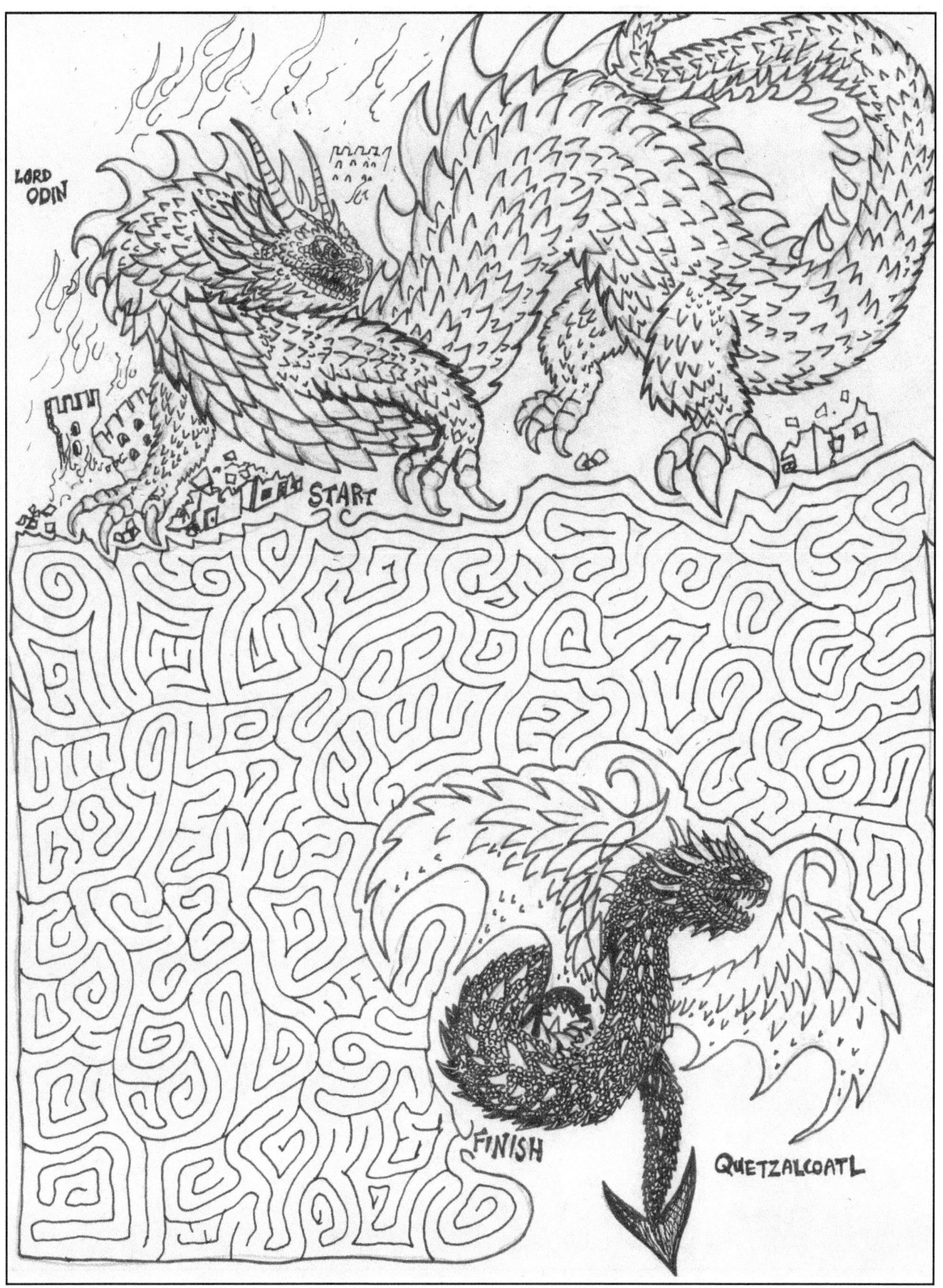

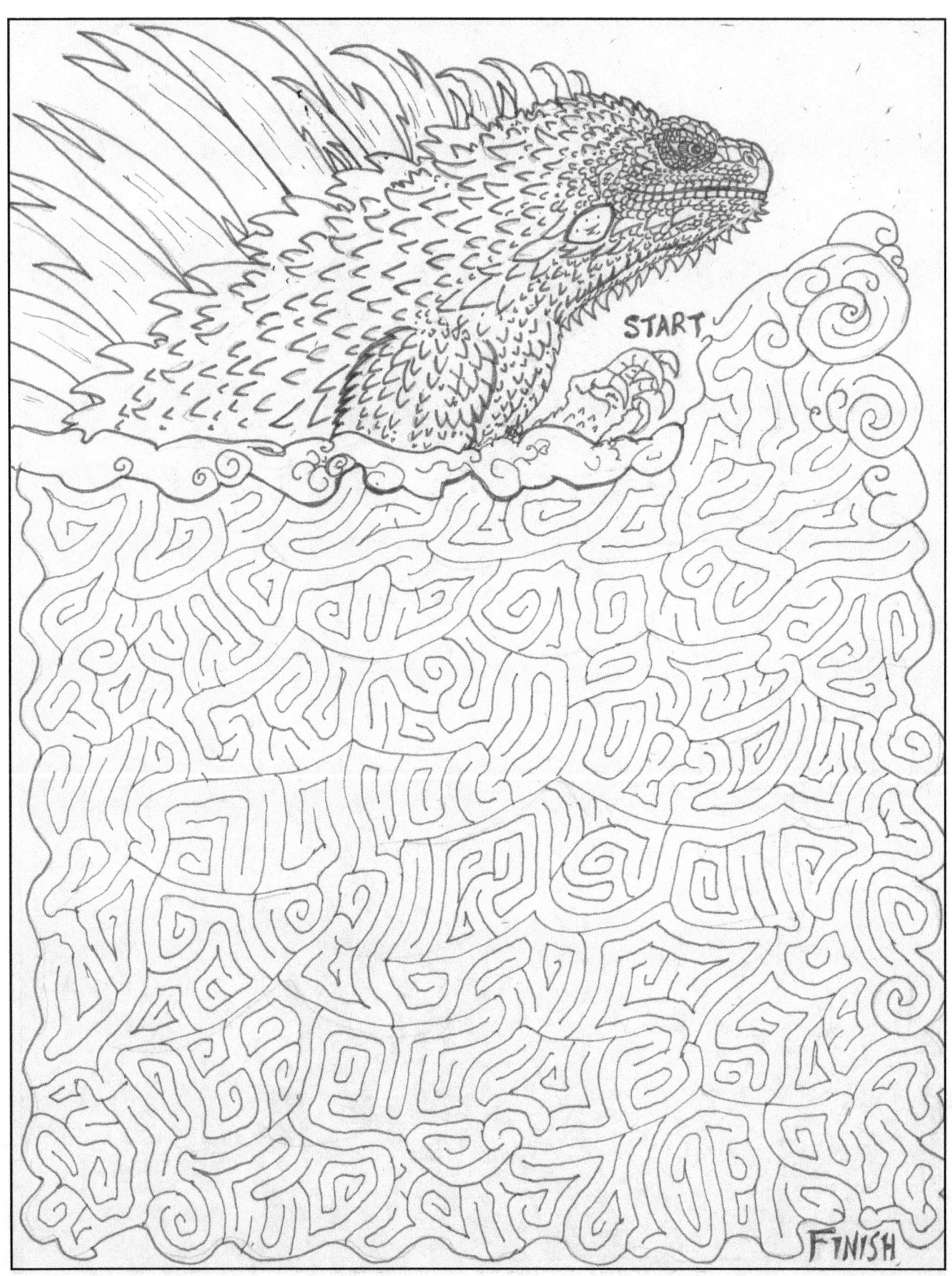

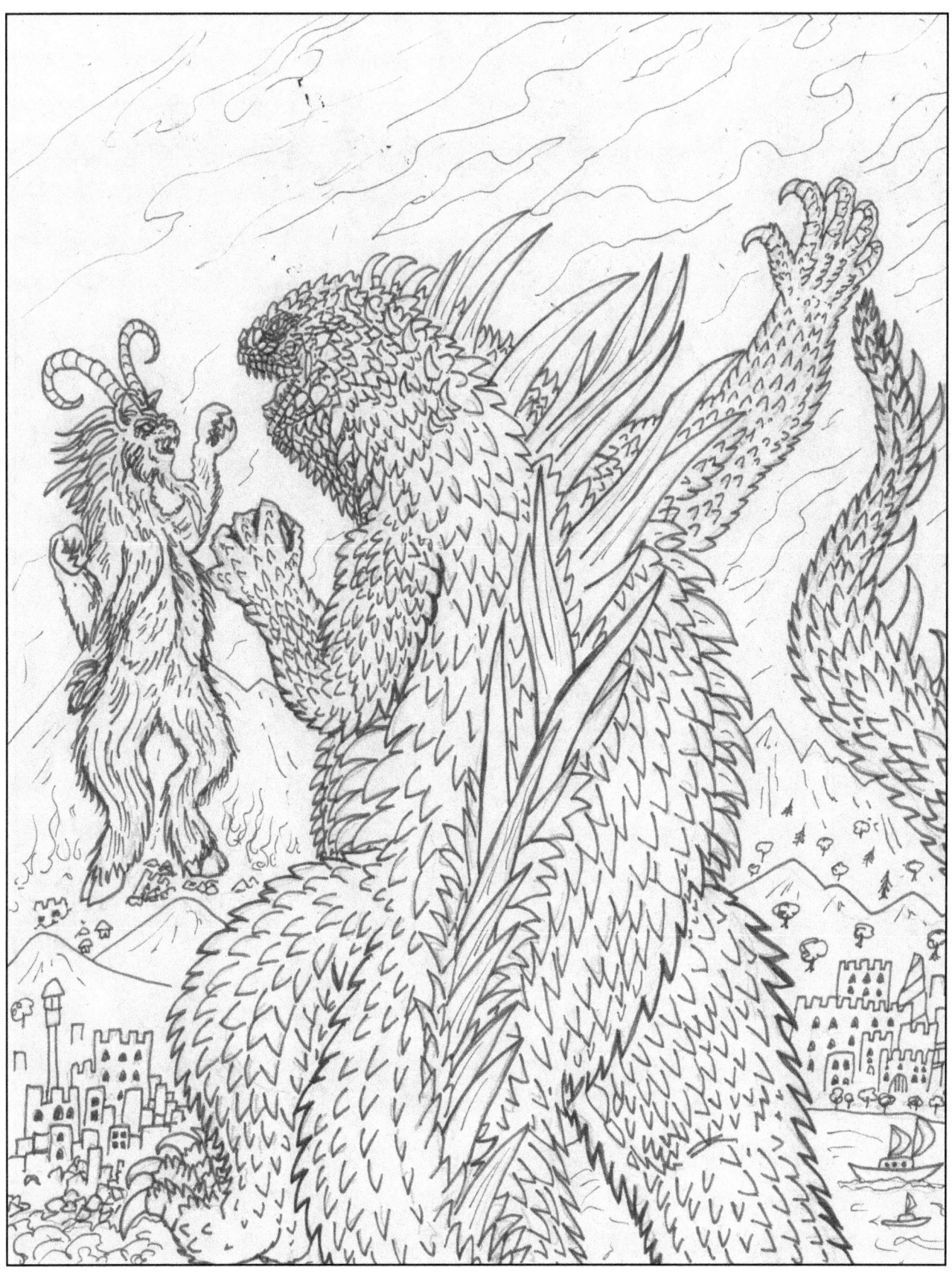

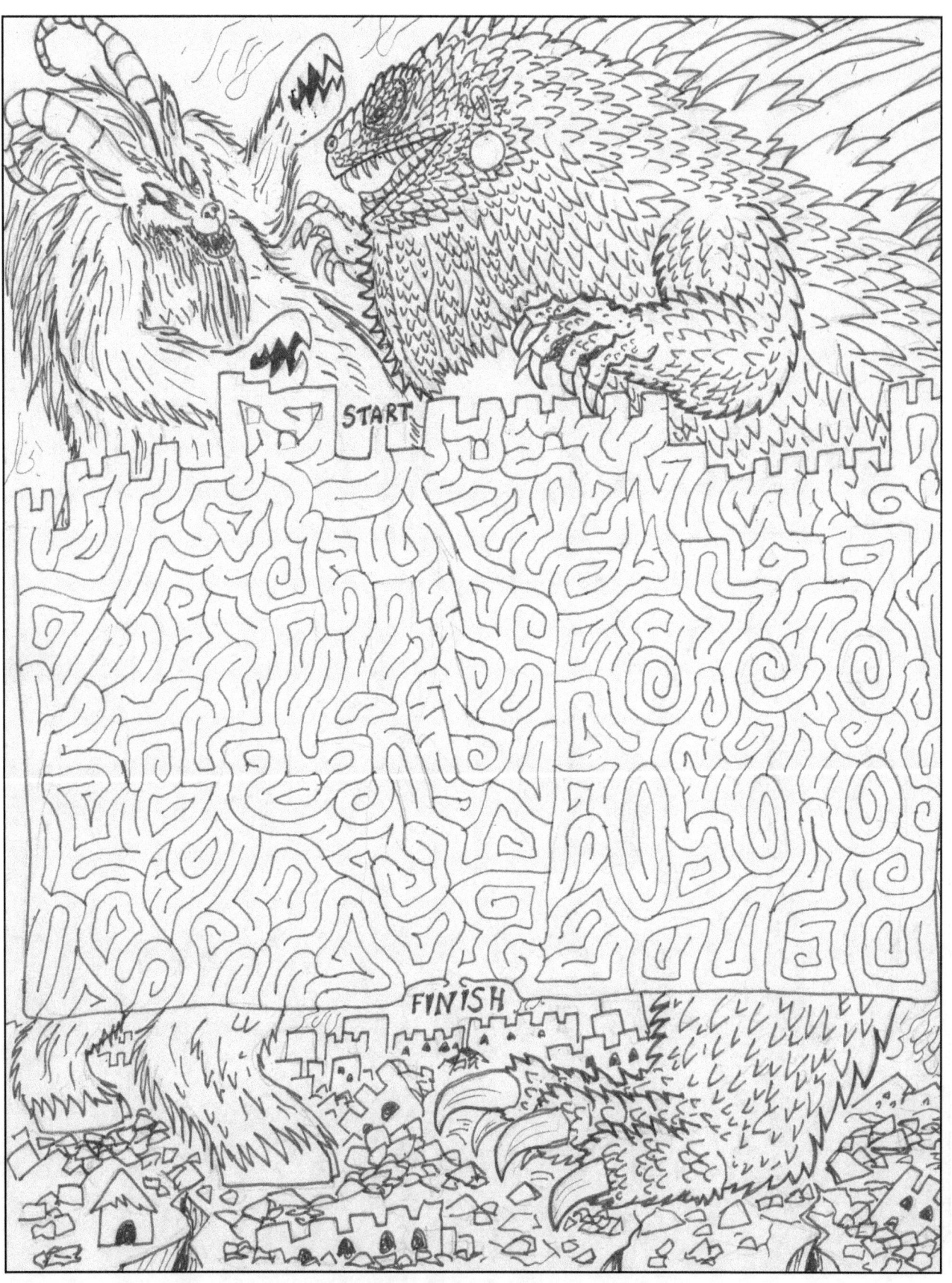

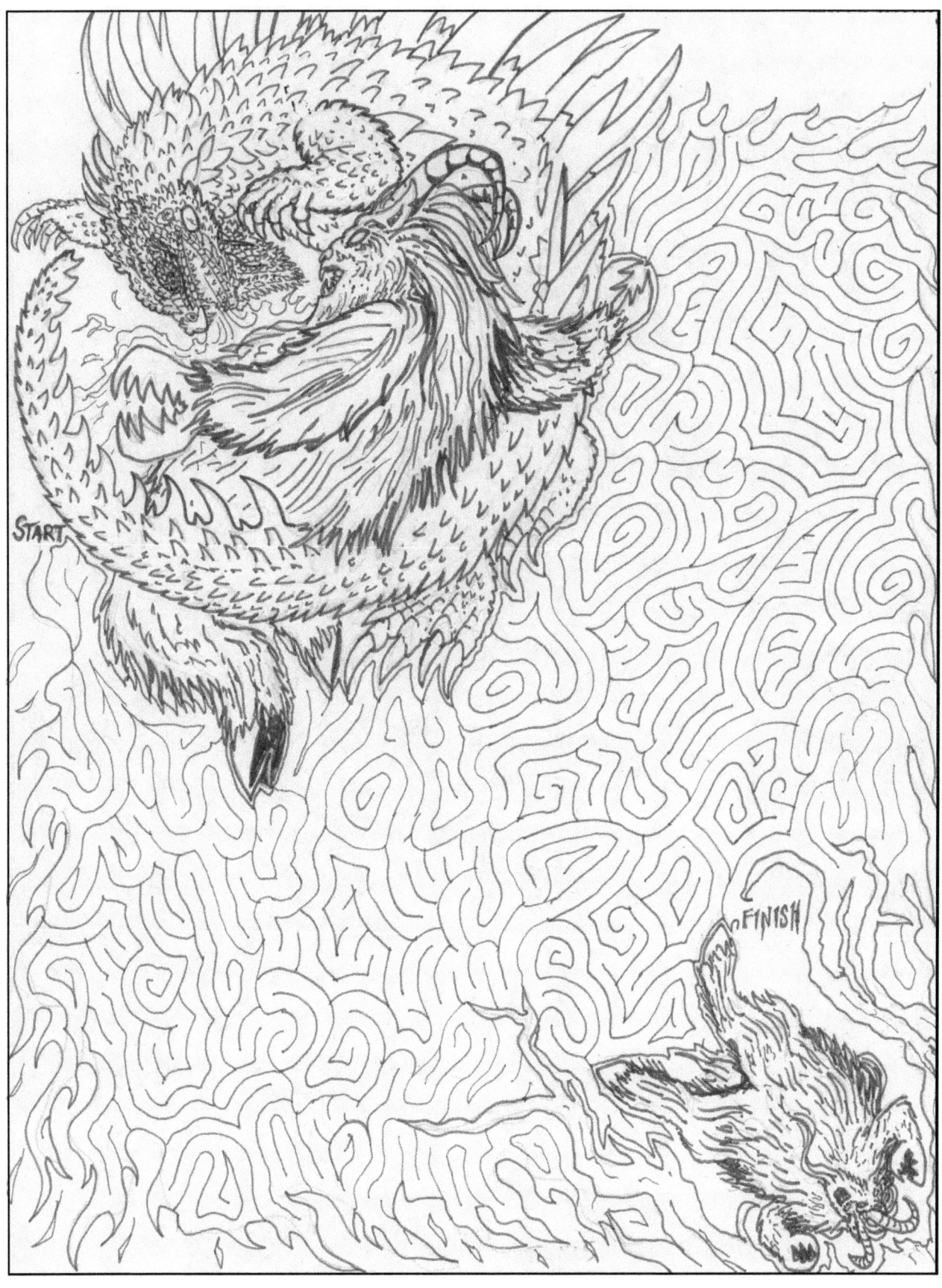

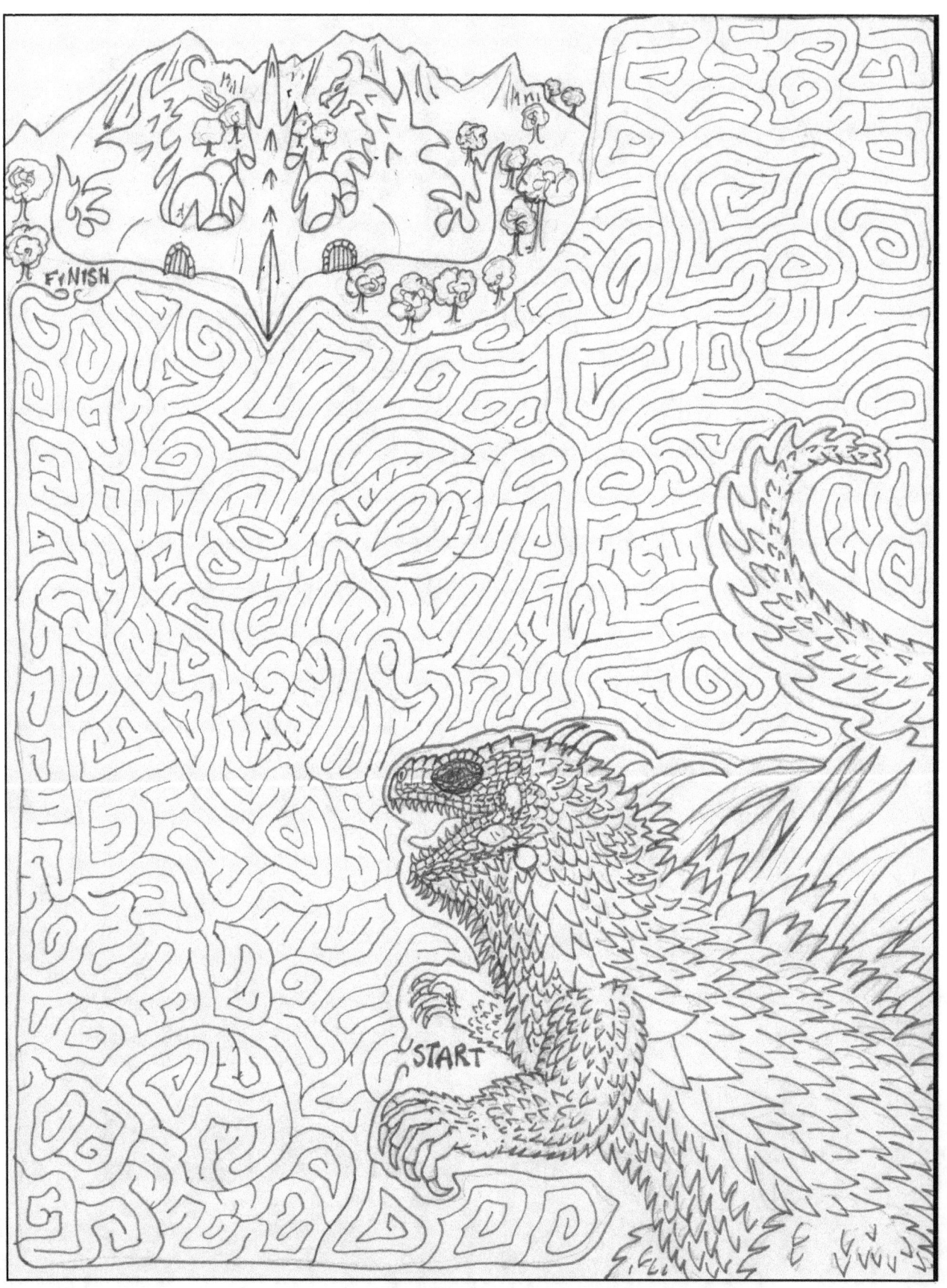

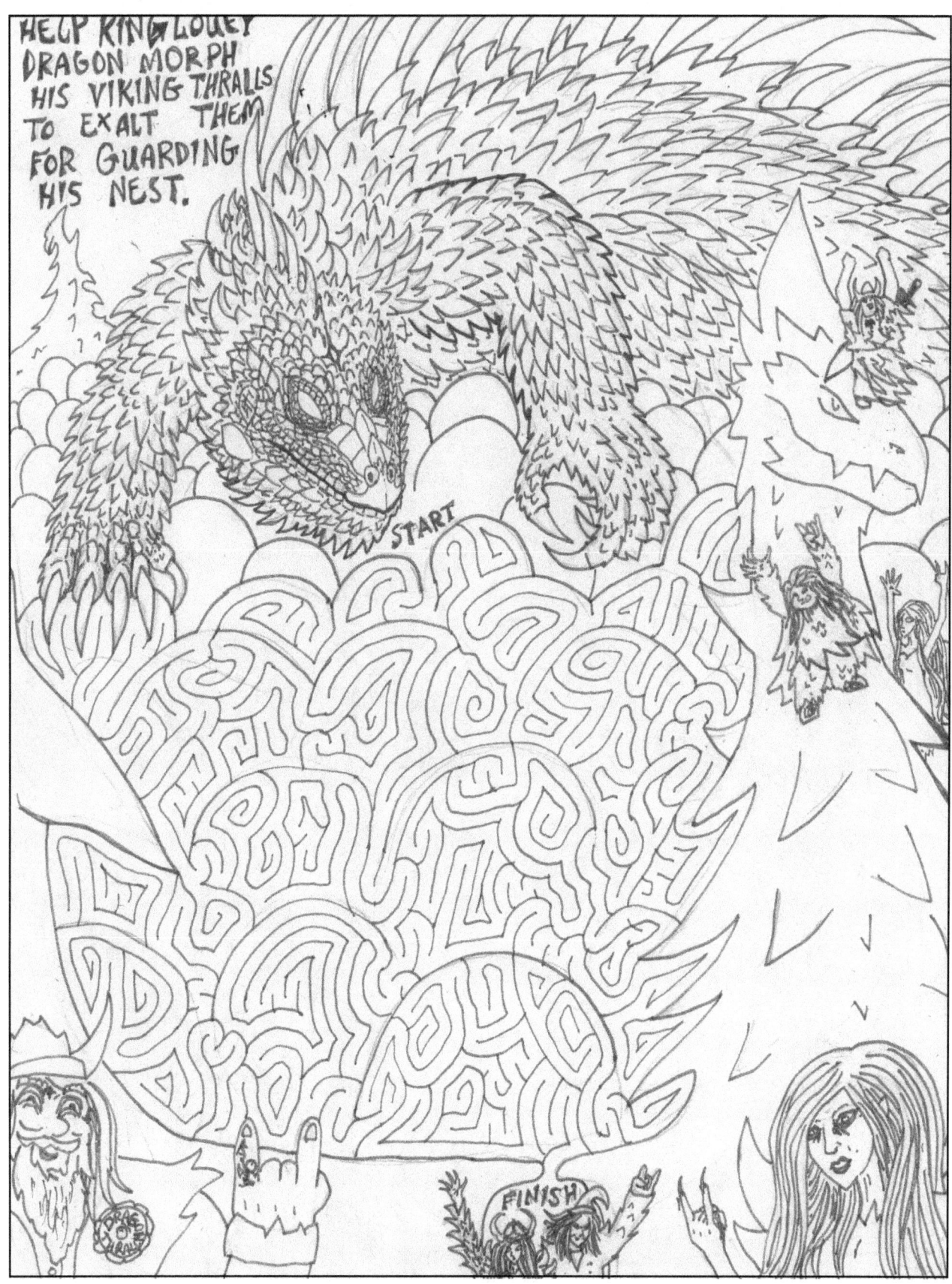

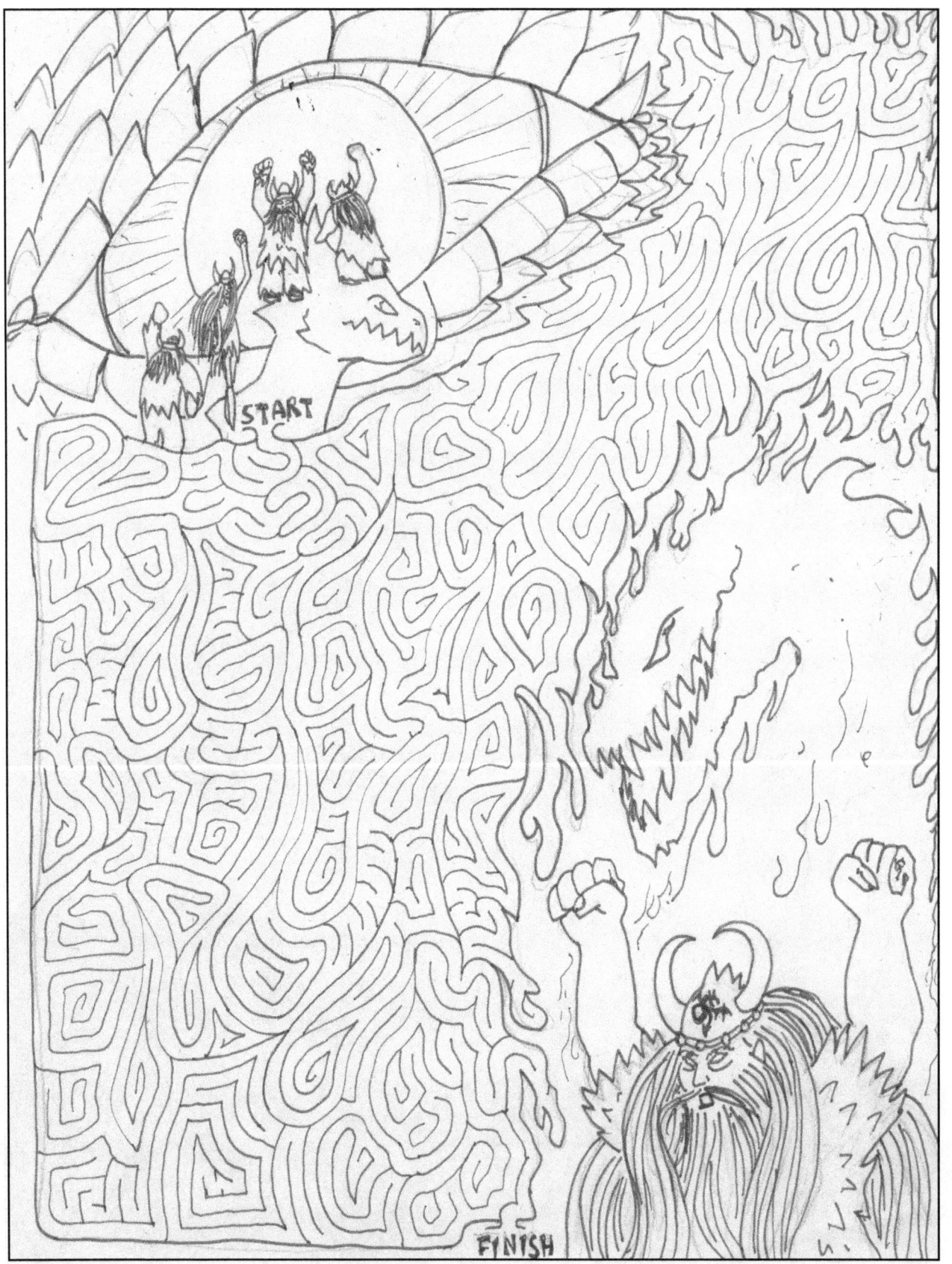

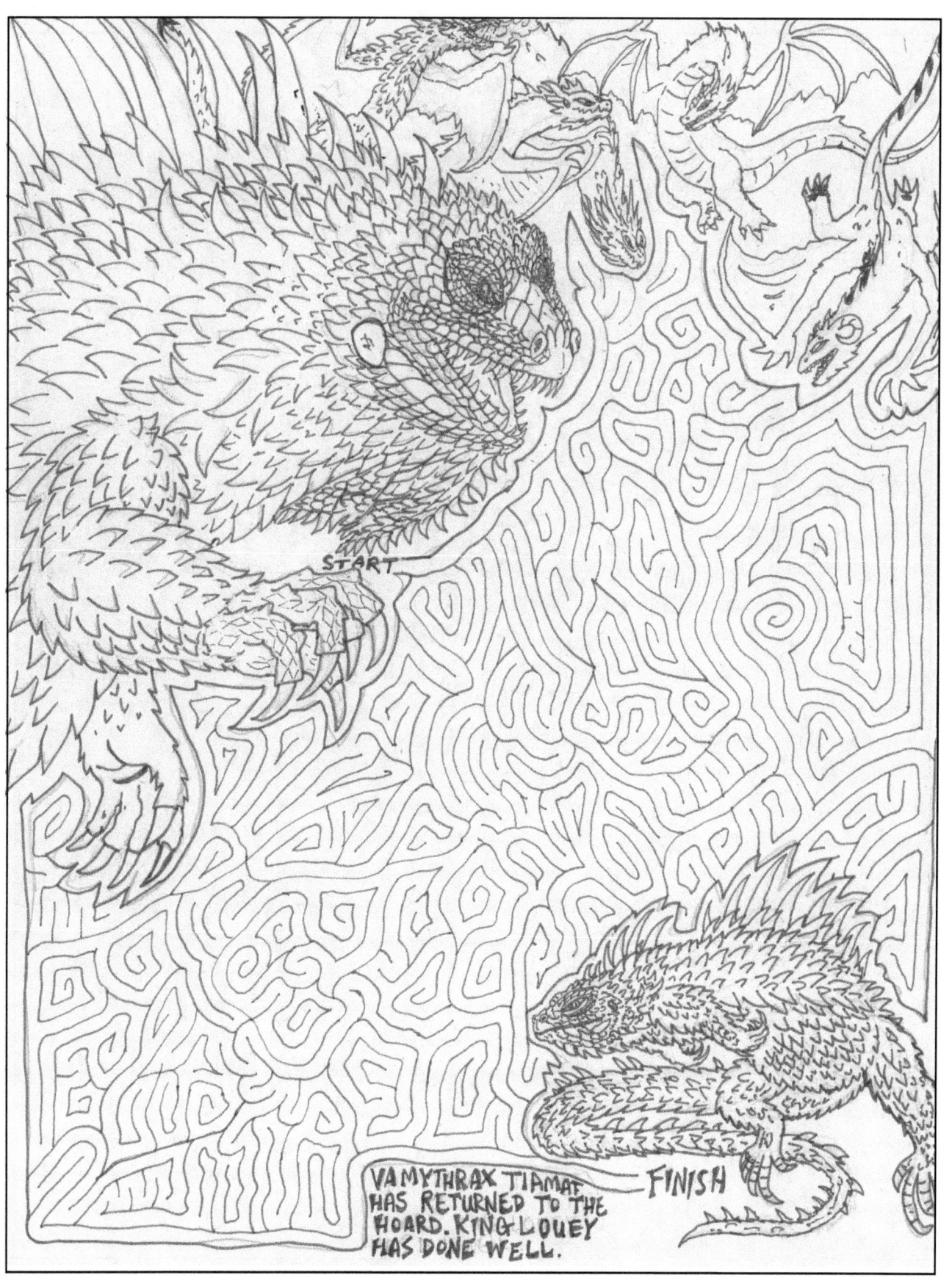

START

FINISH

VA MYTHRAX TIAMAT
HAS RETURNED TO THE
HOARD. KING LOUEY
HAS DONE WELL.

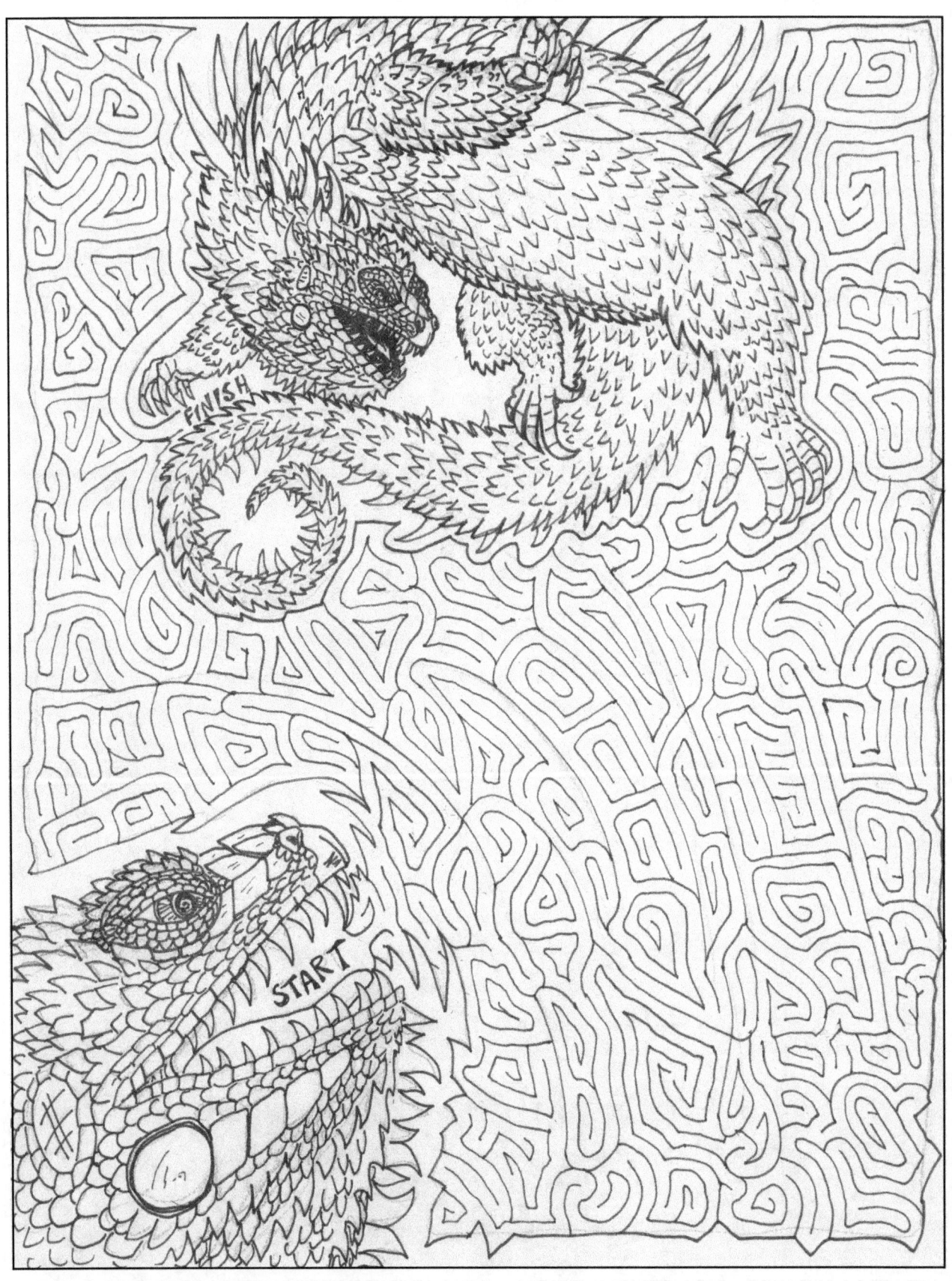

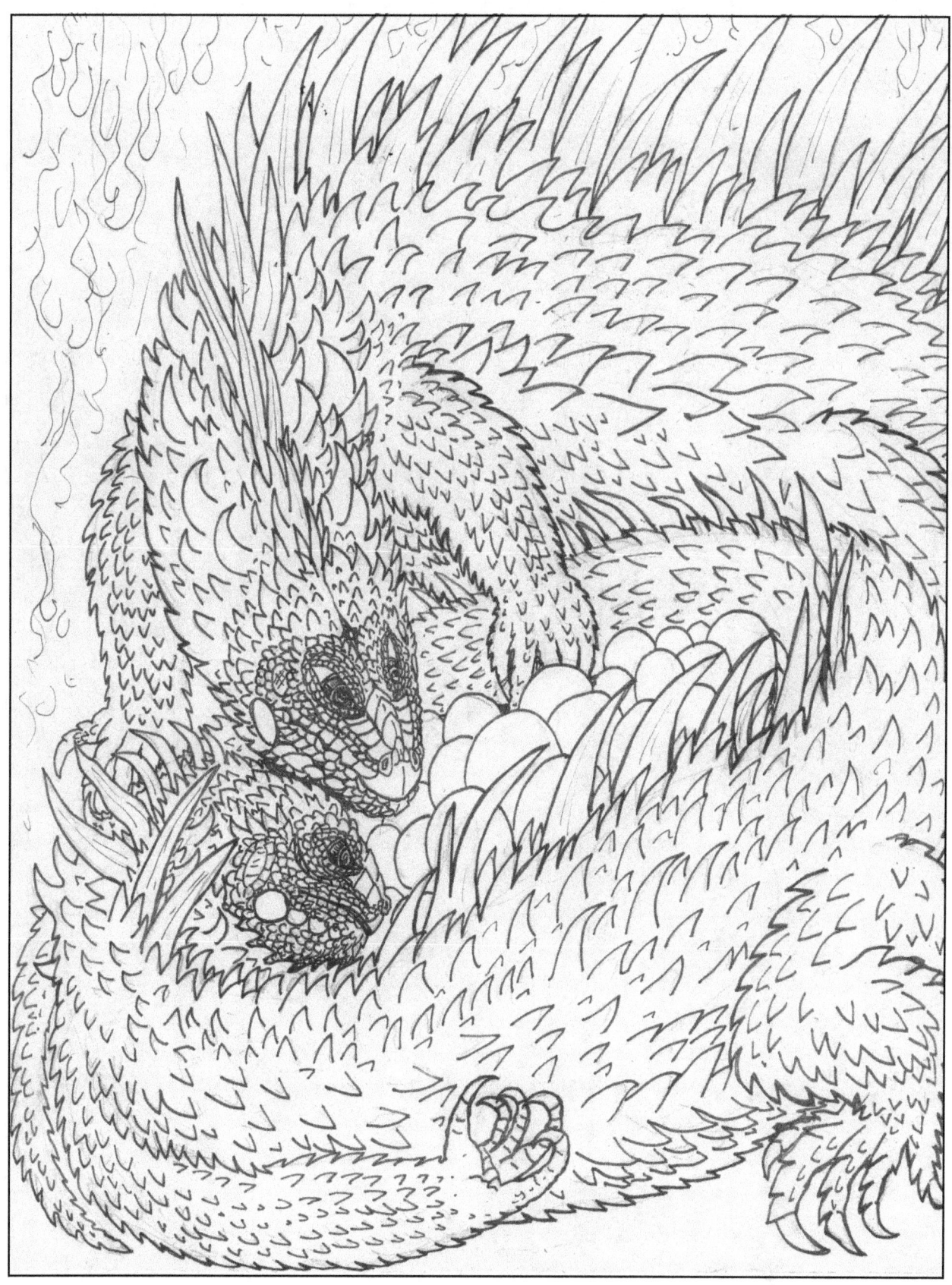

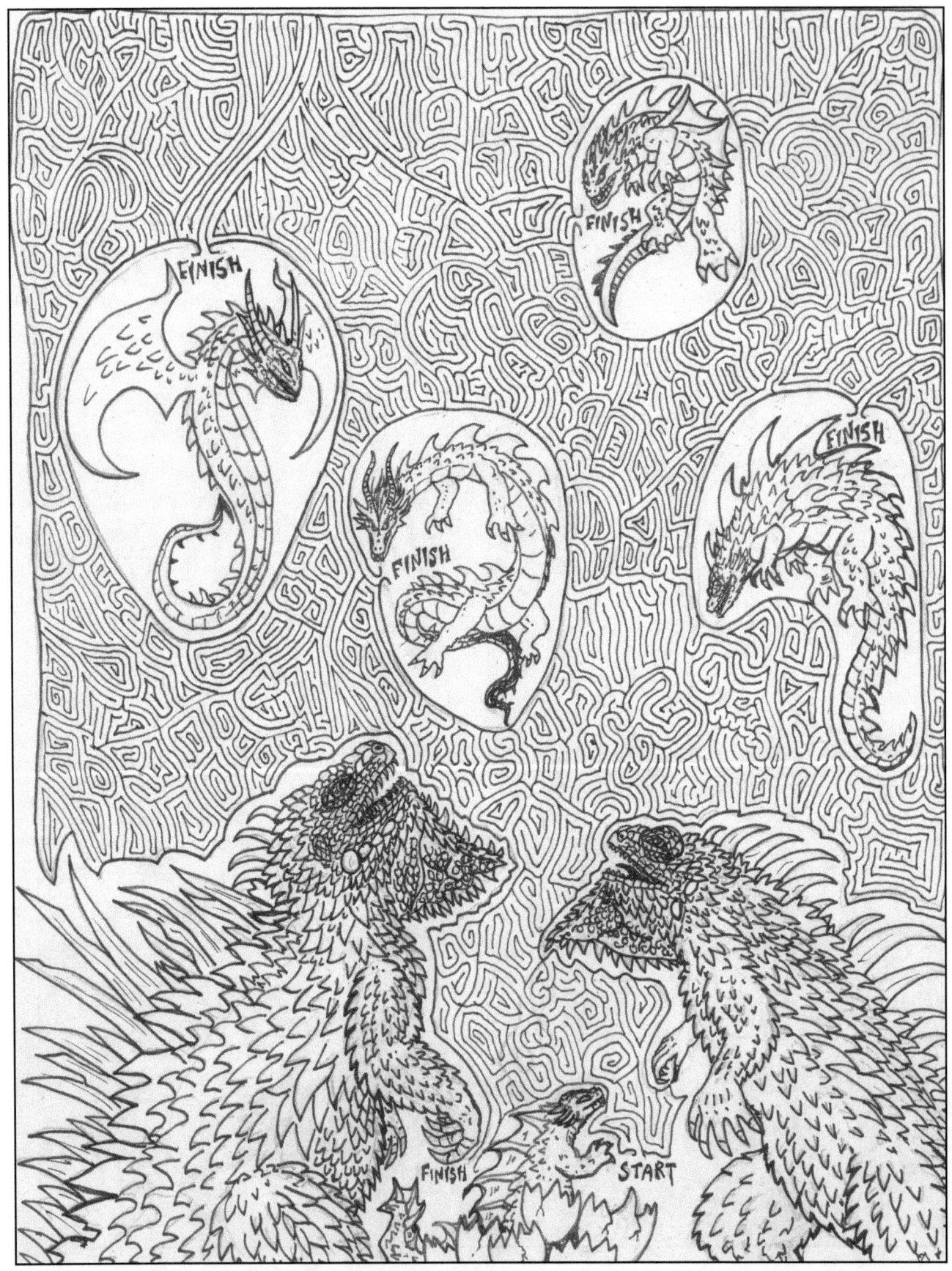

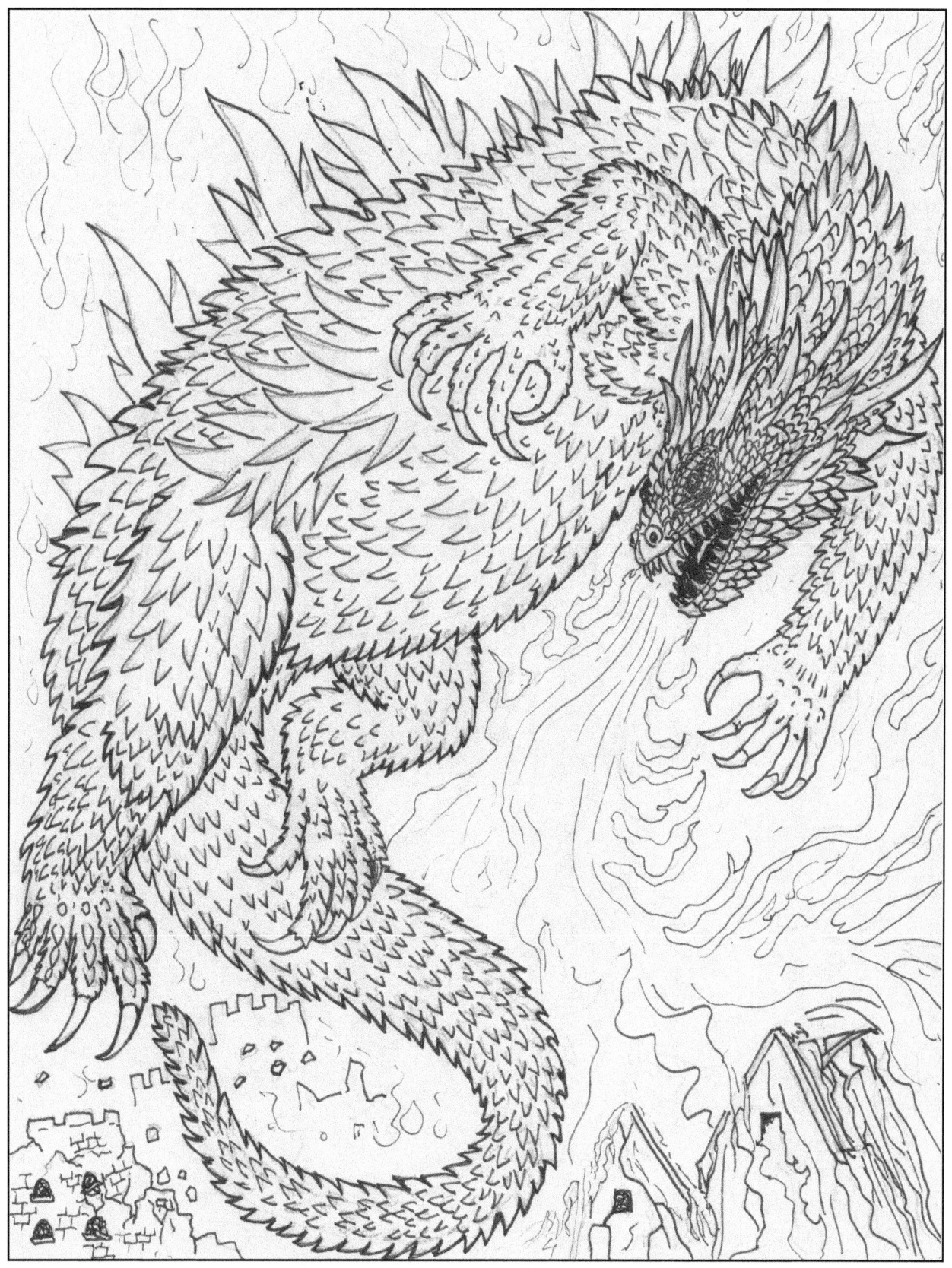

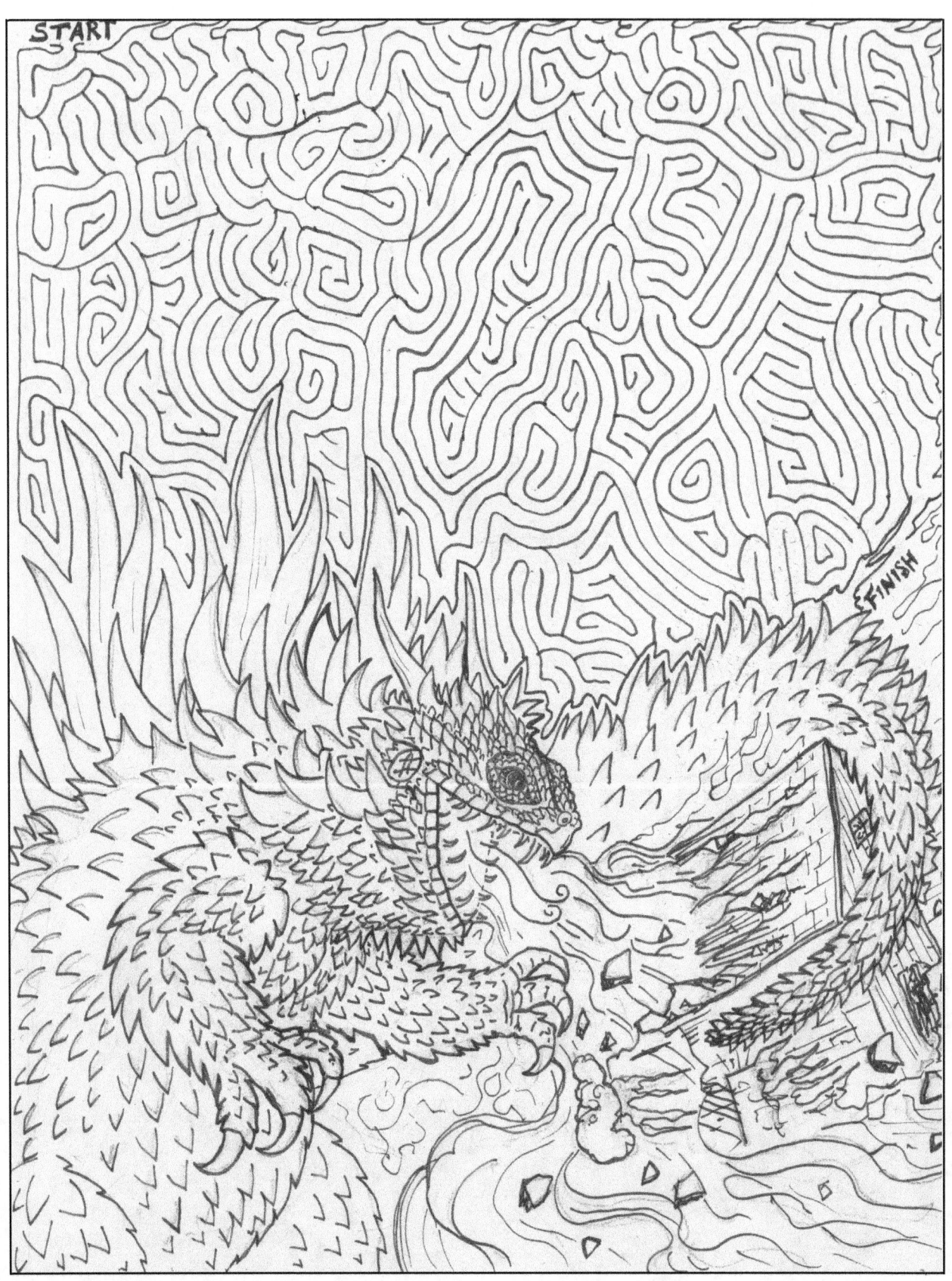

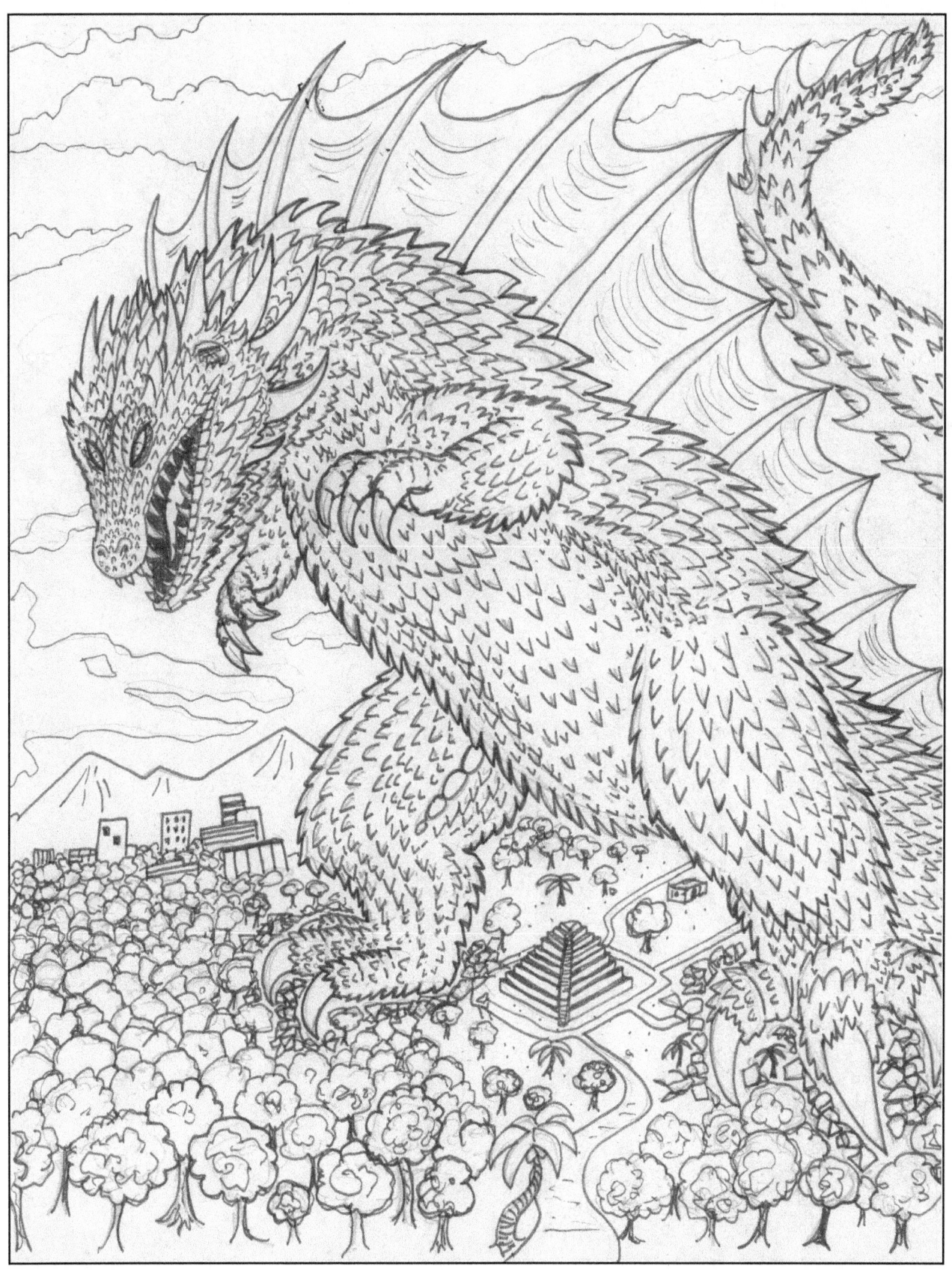

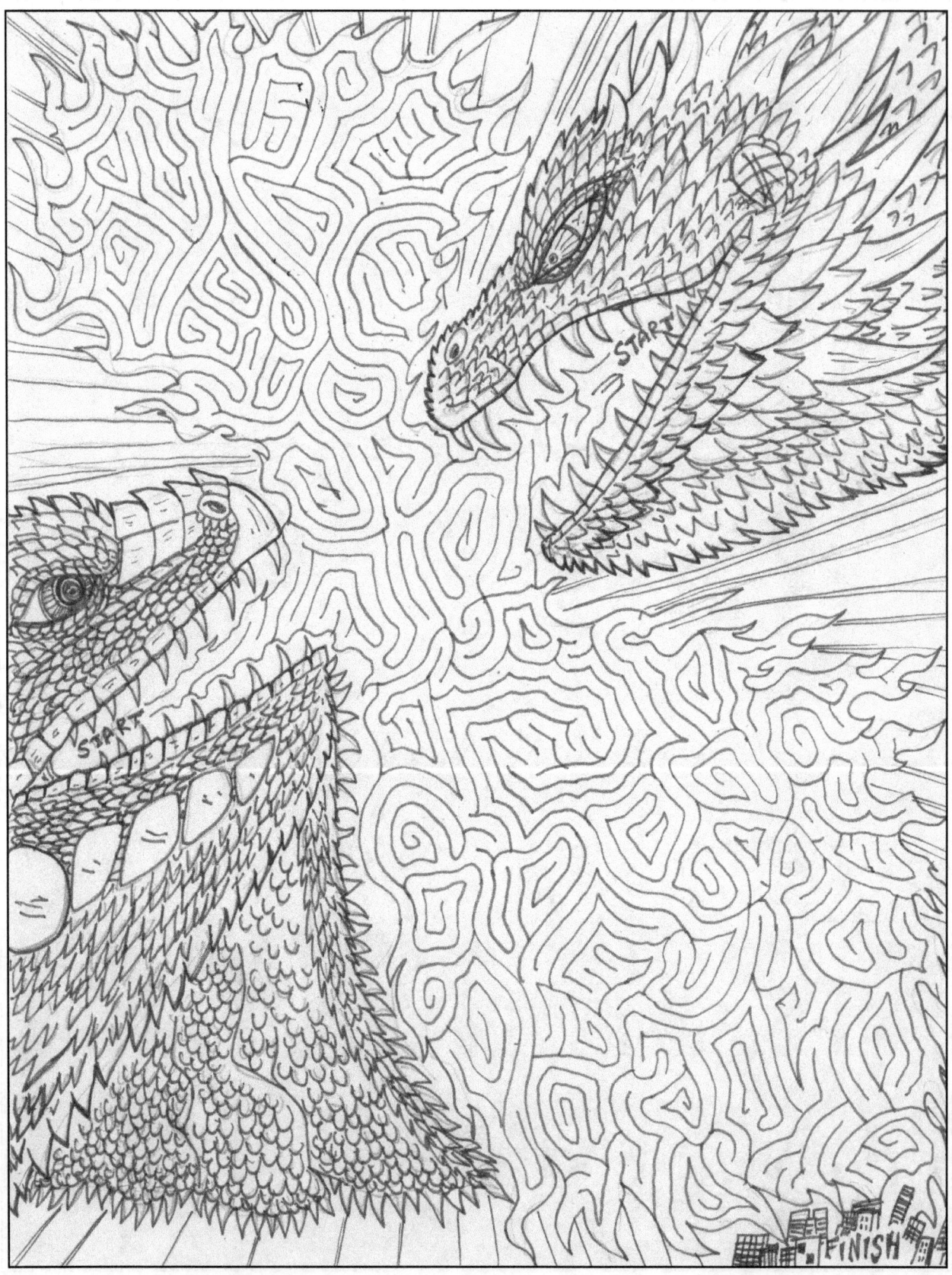

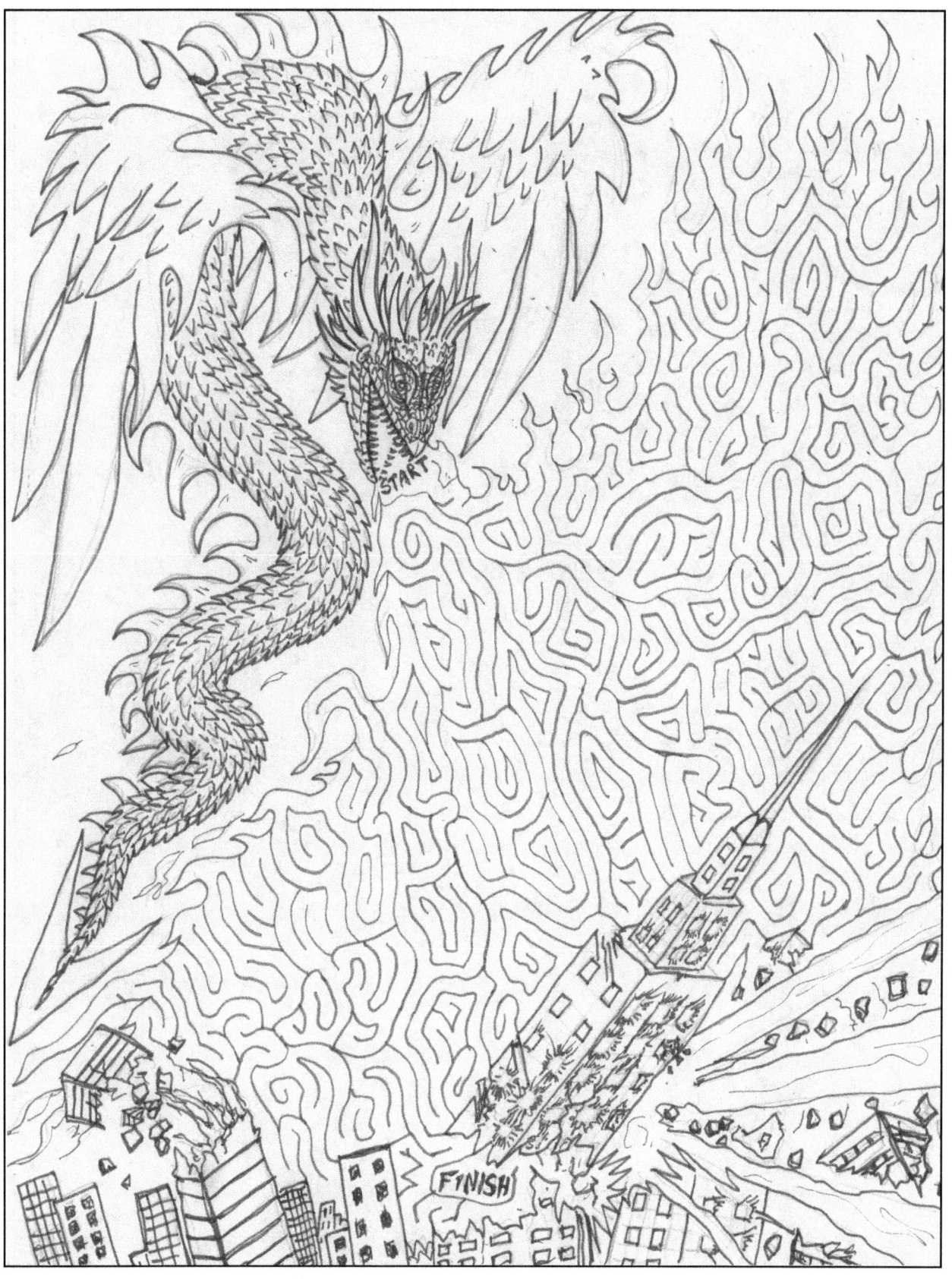

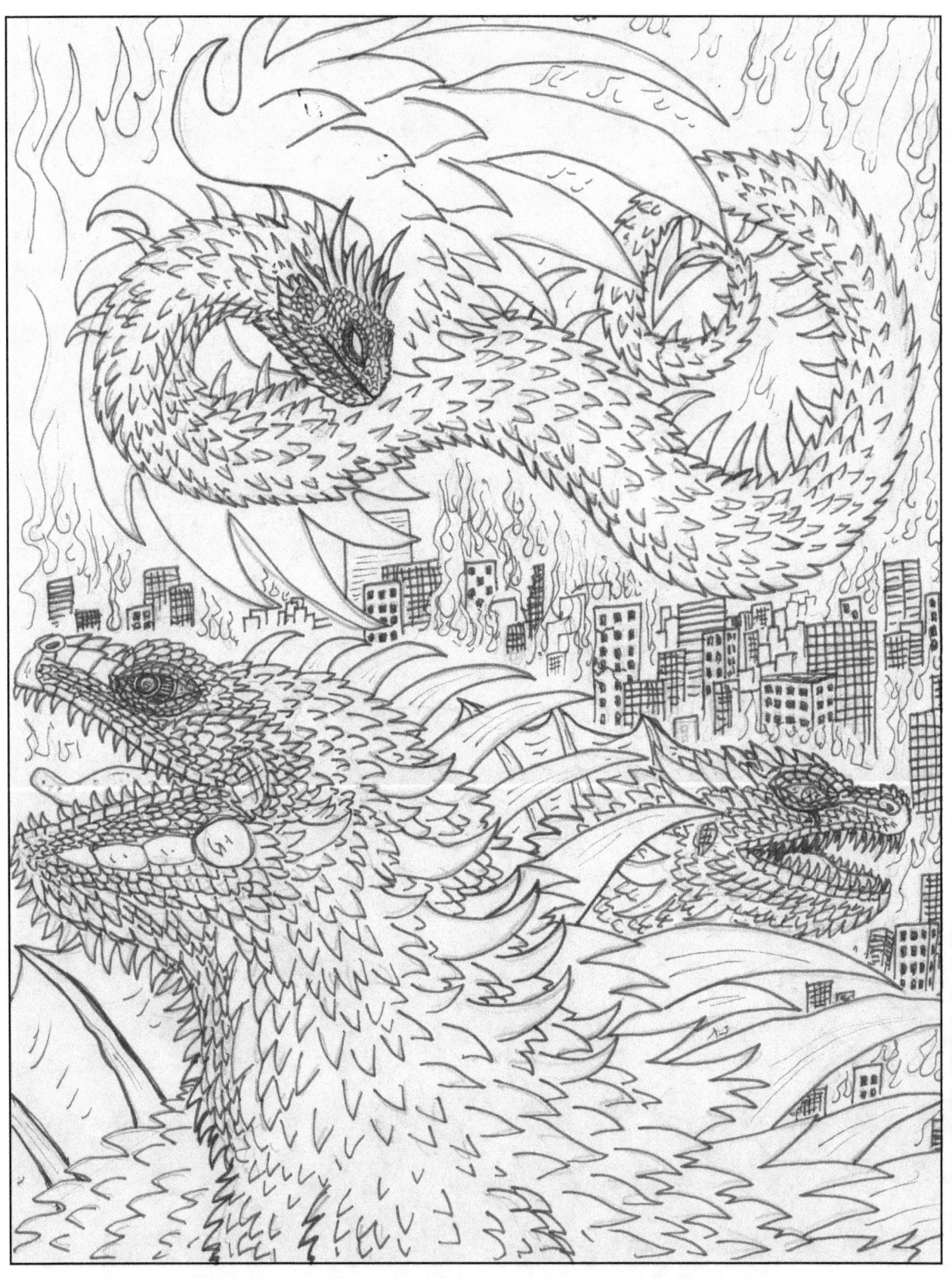

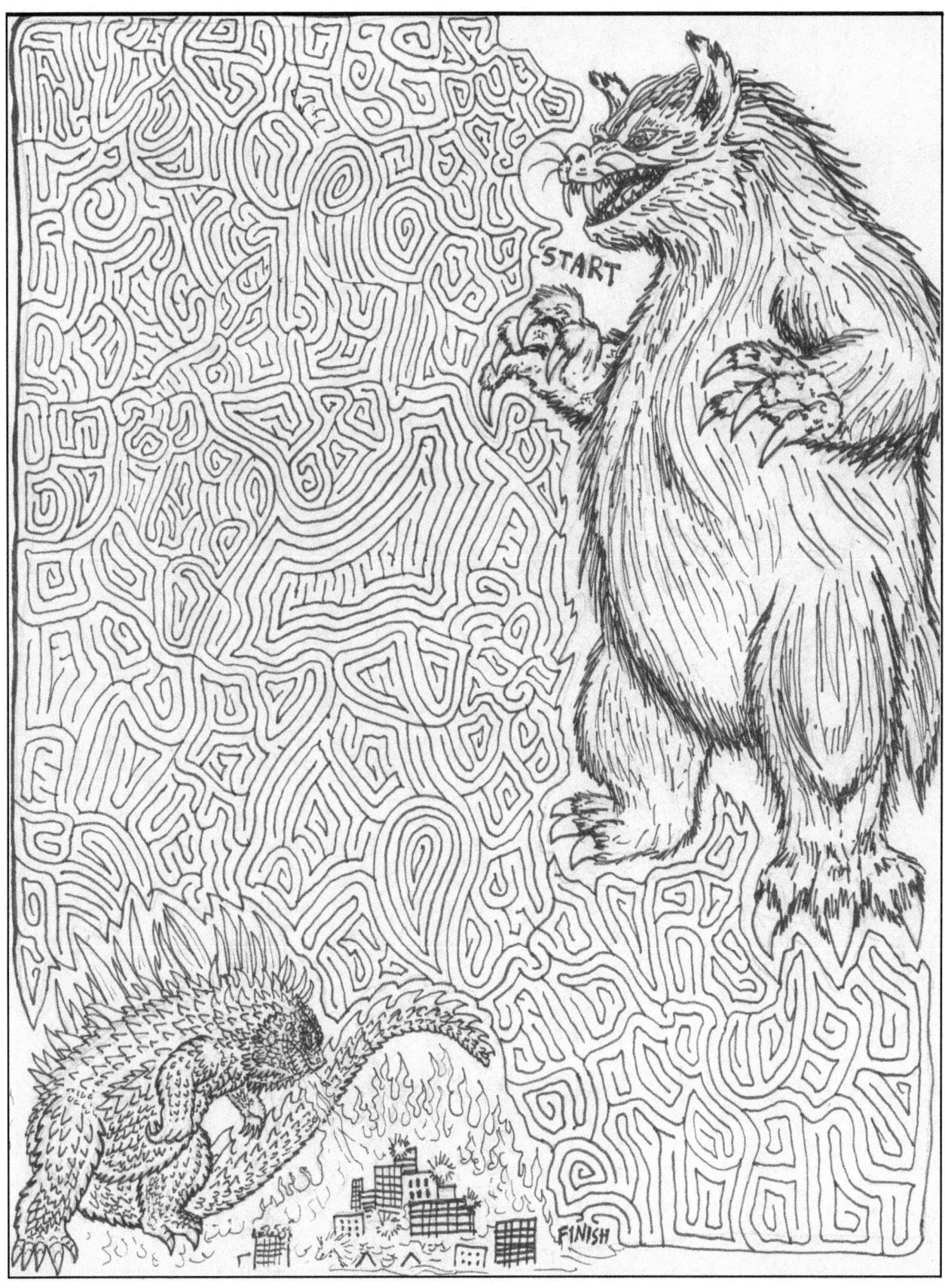

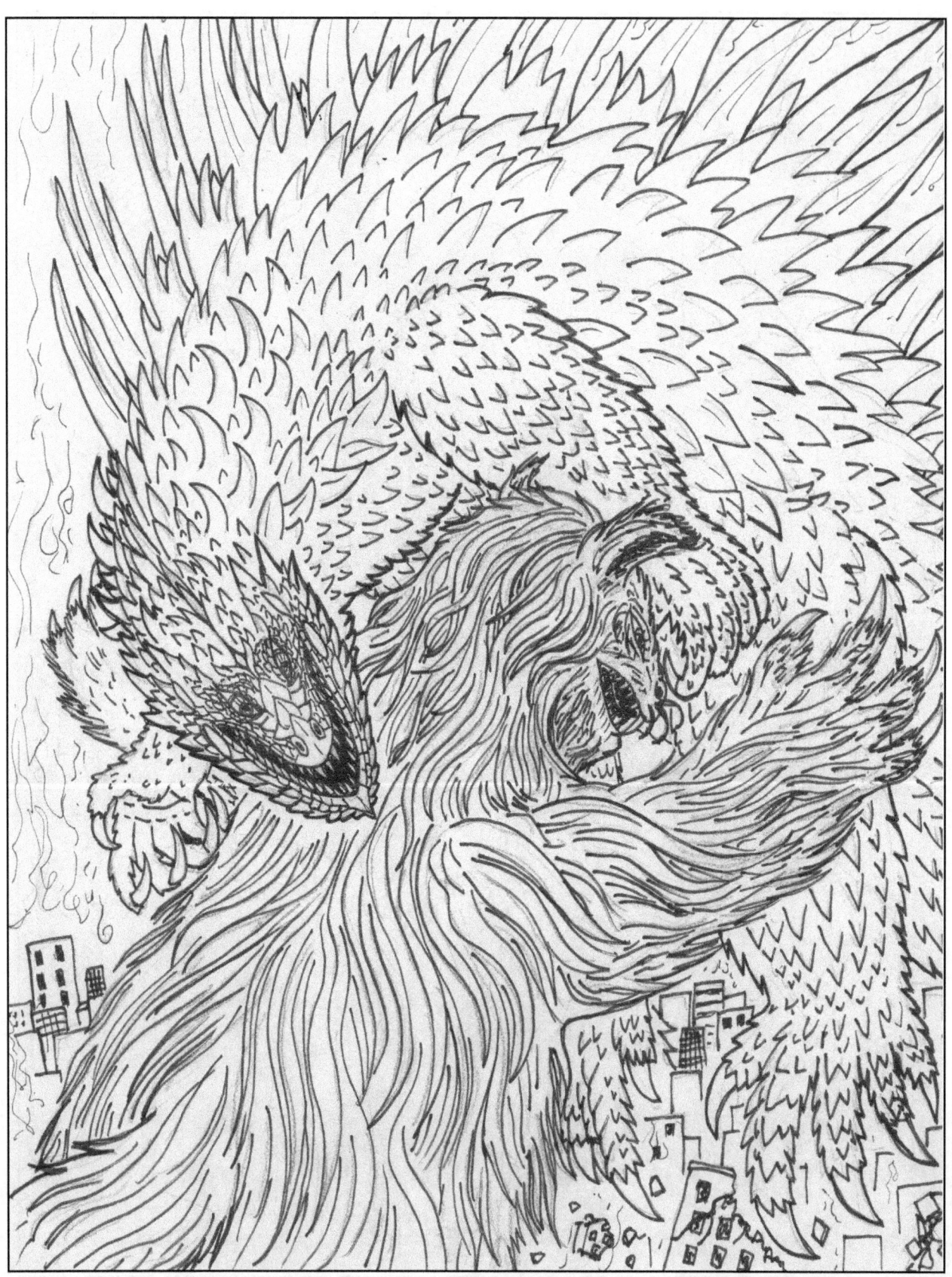

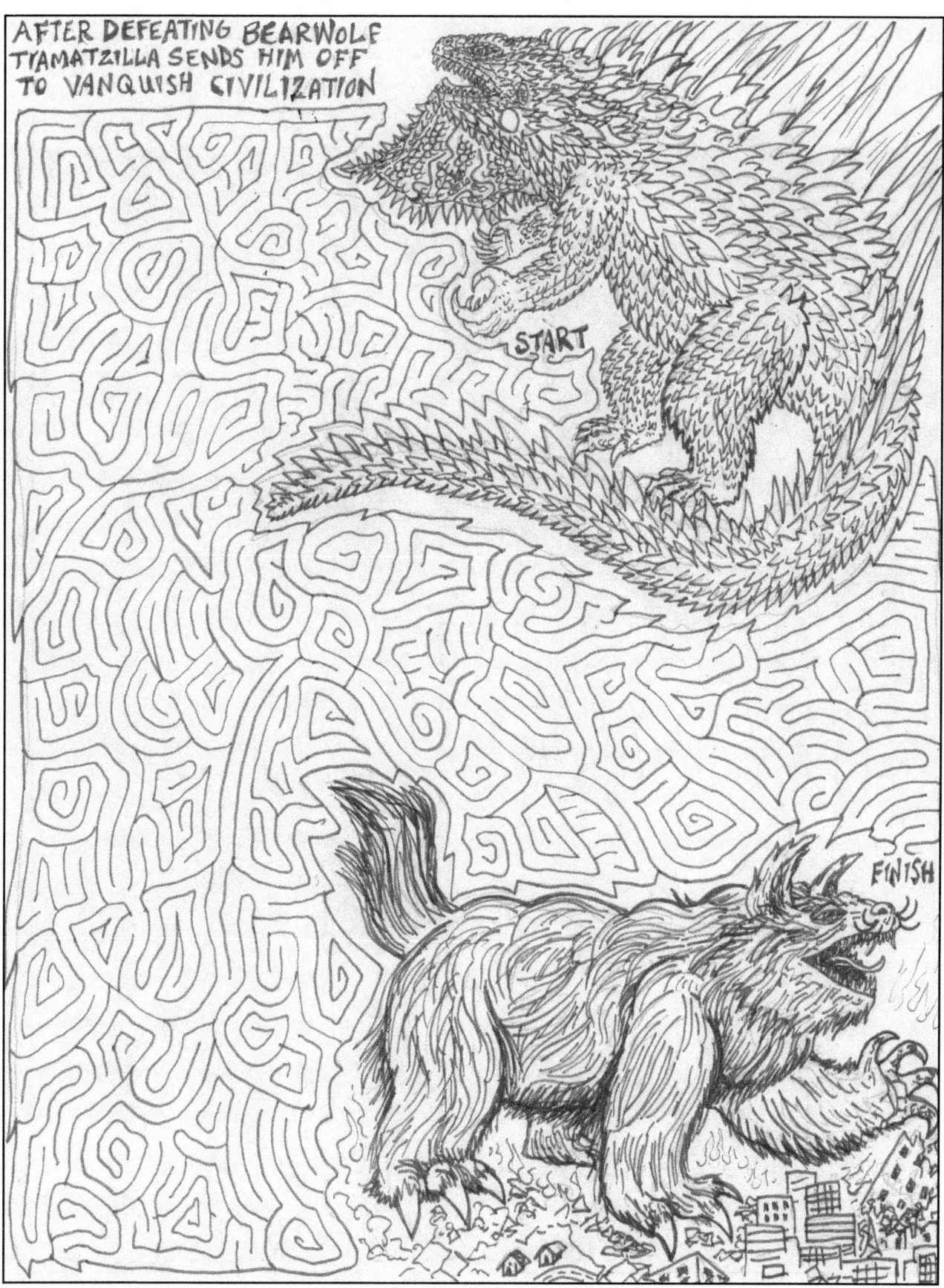

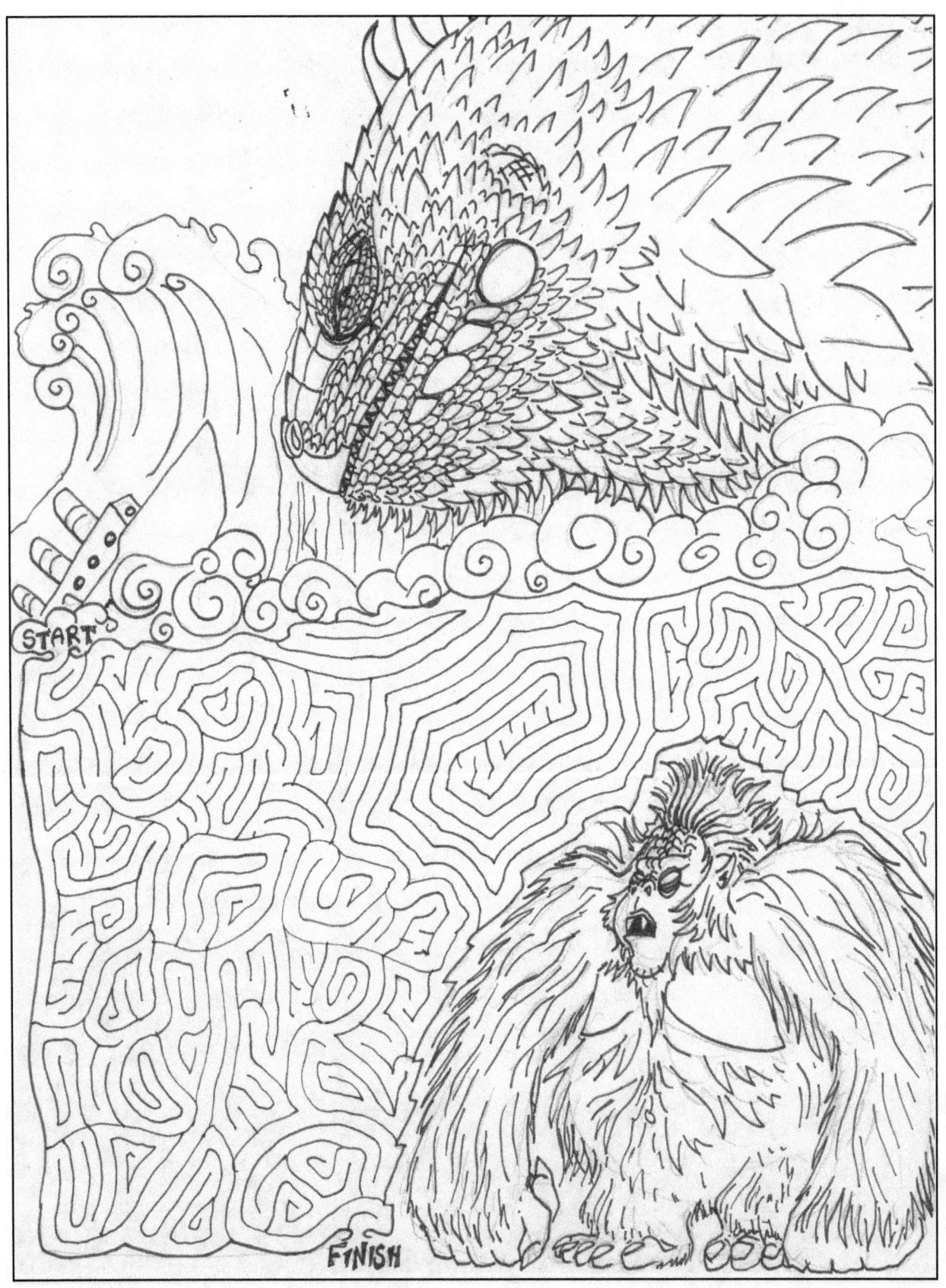

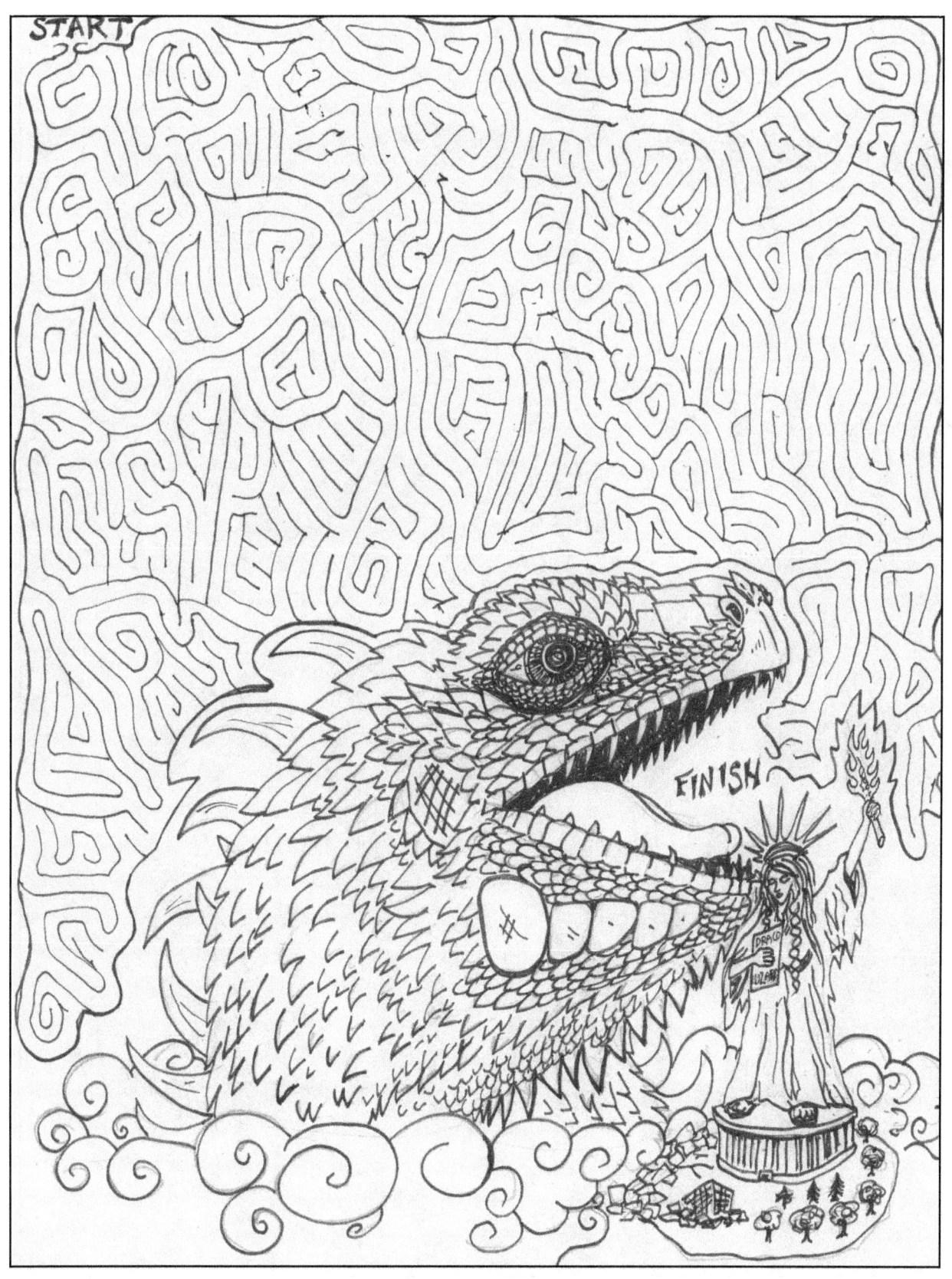

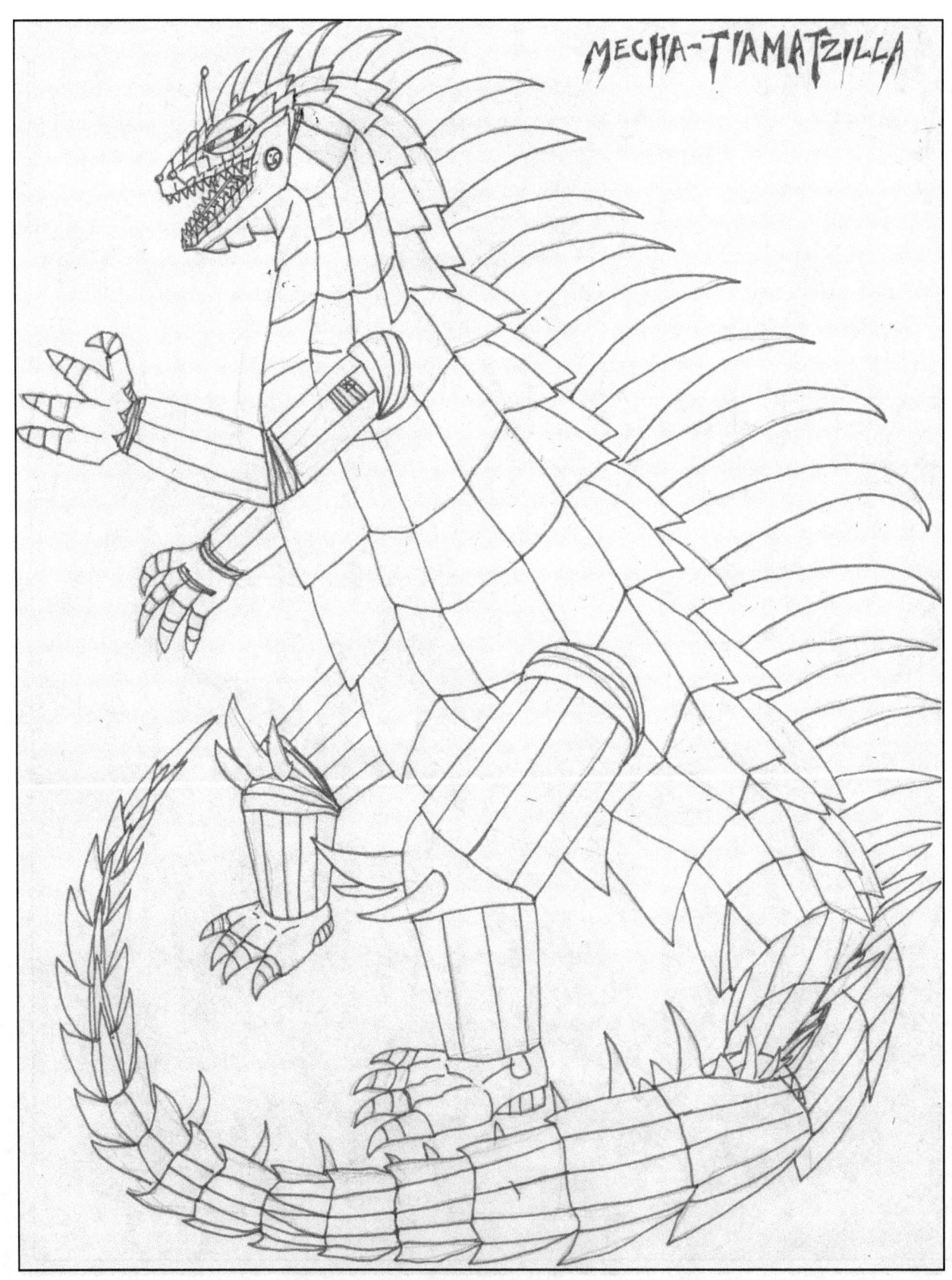

MECHA-TIAMATZILLA

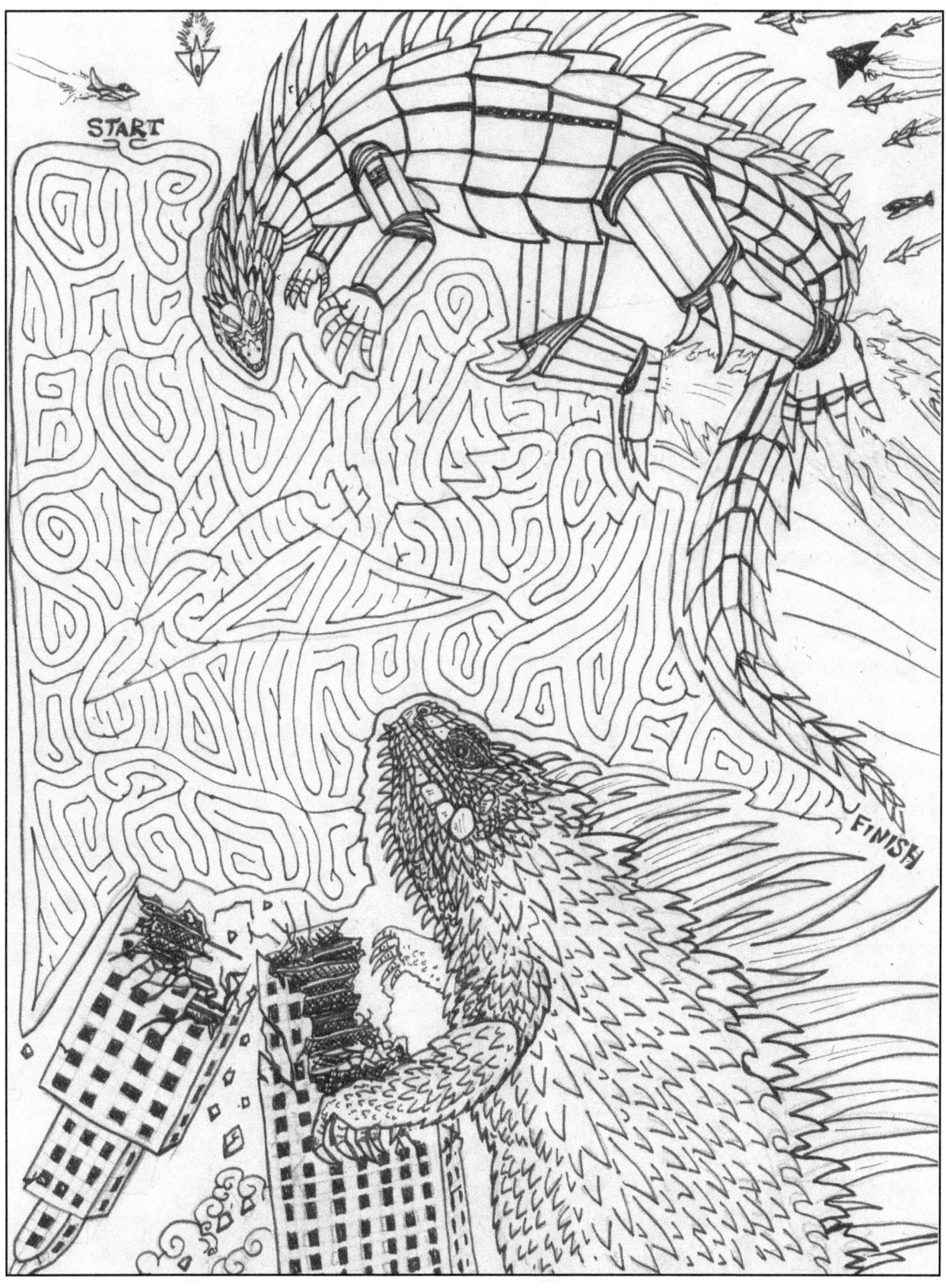

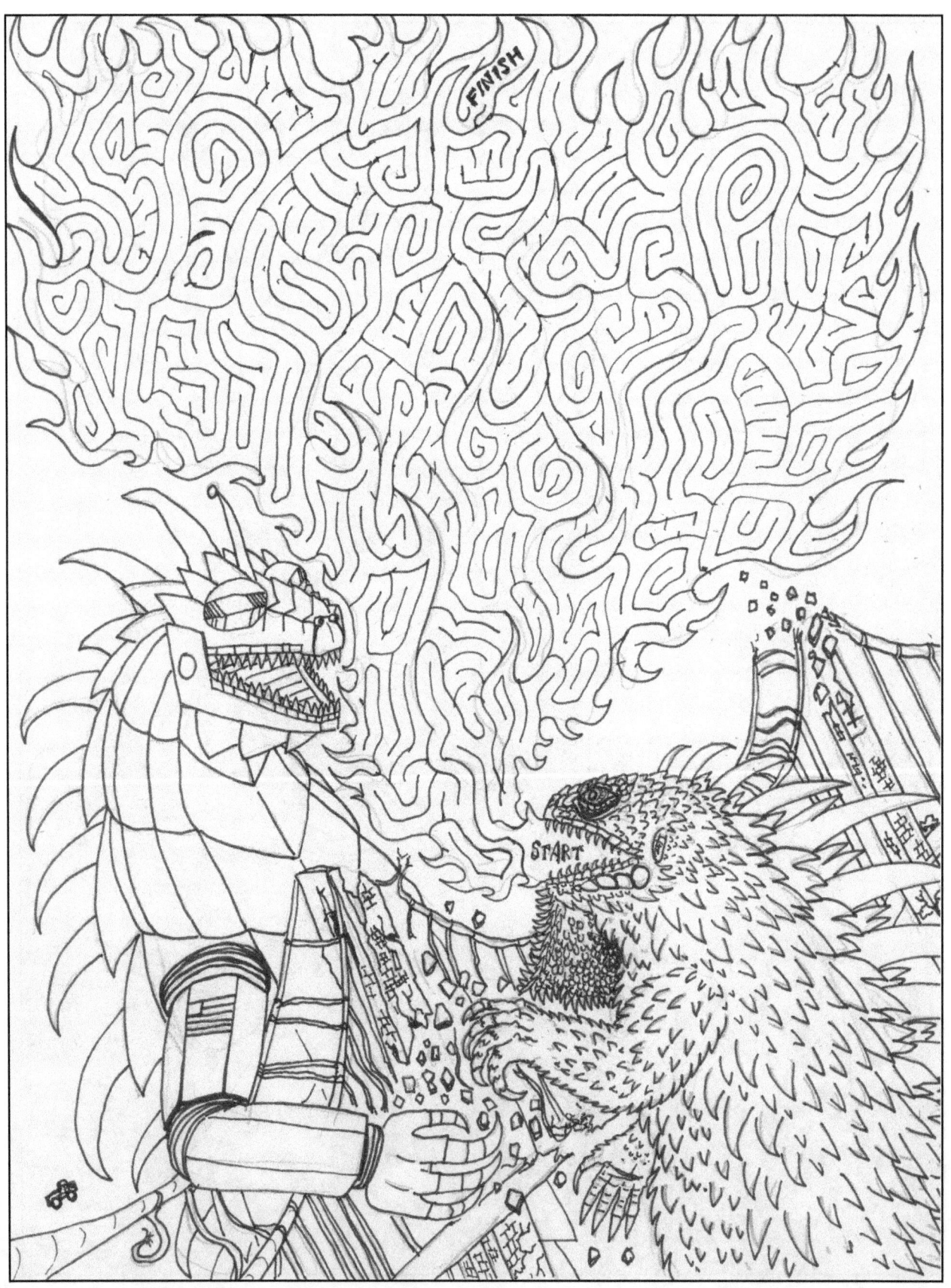

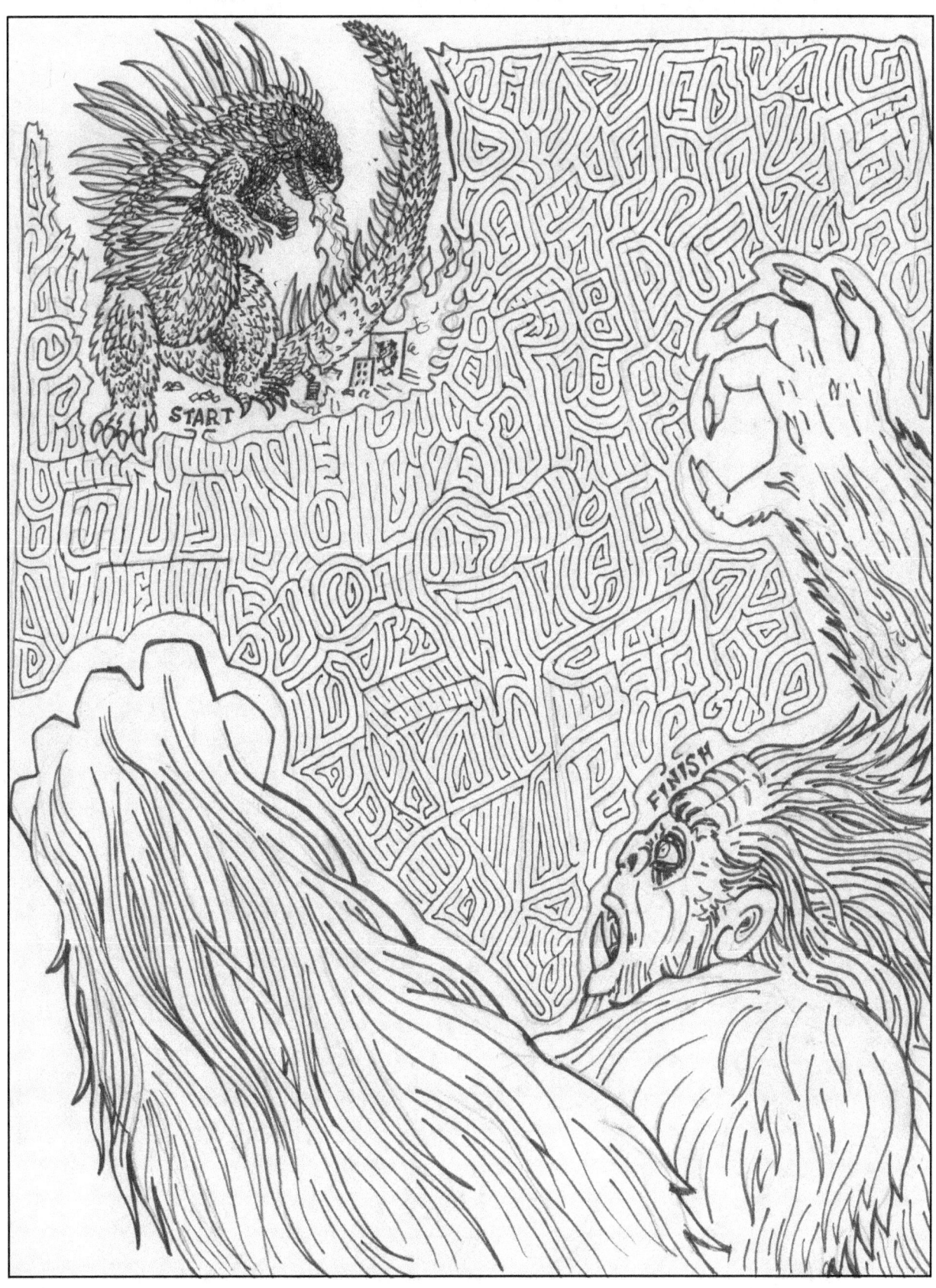

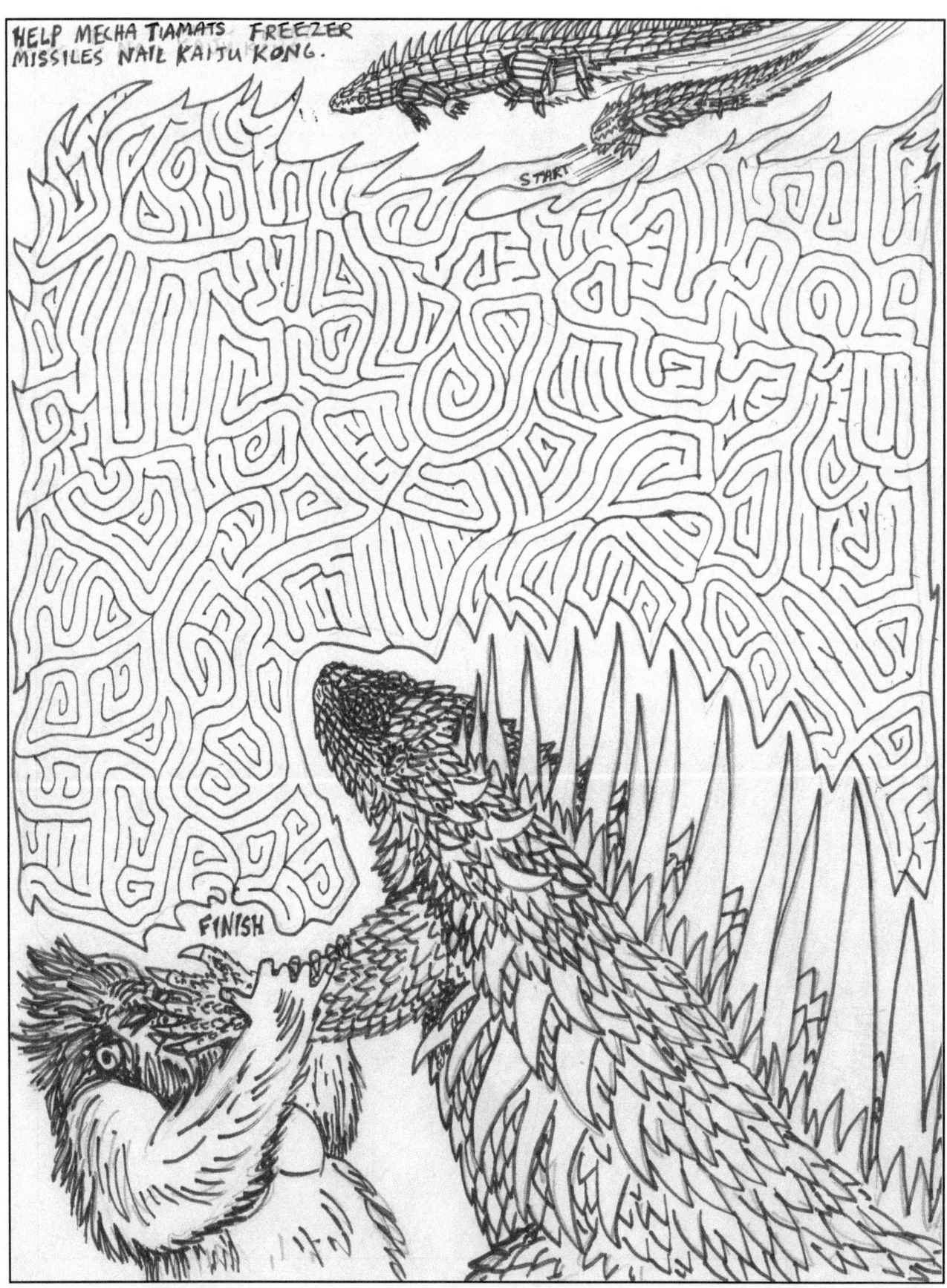

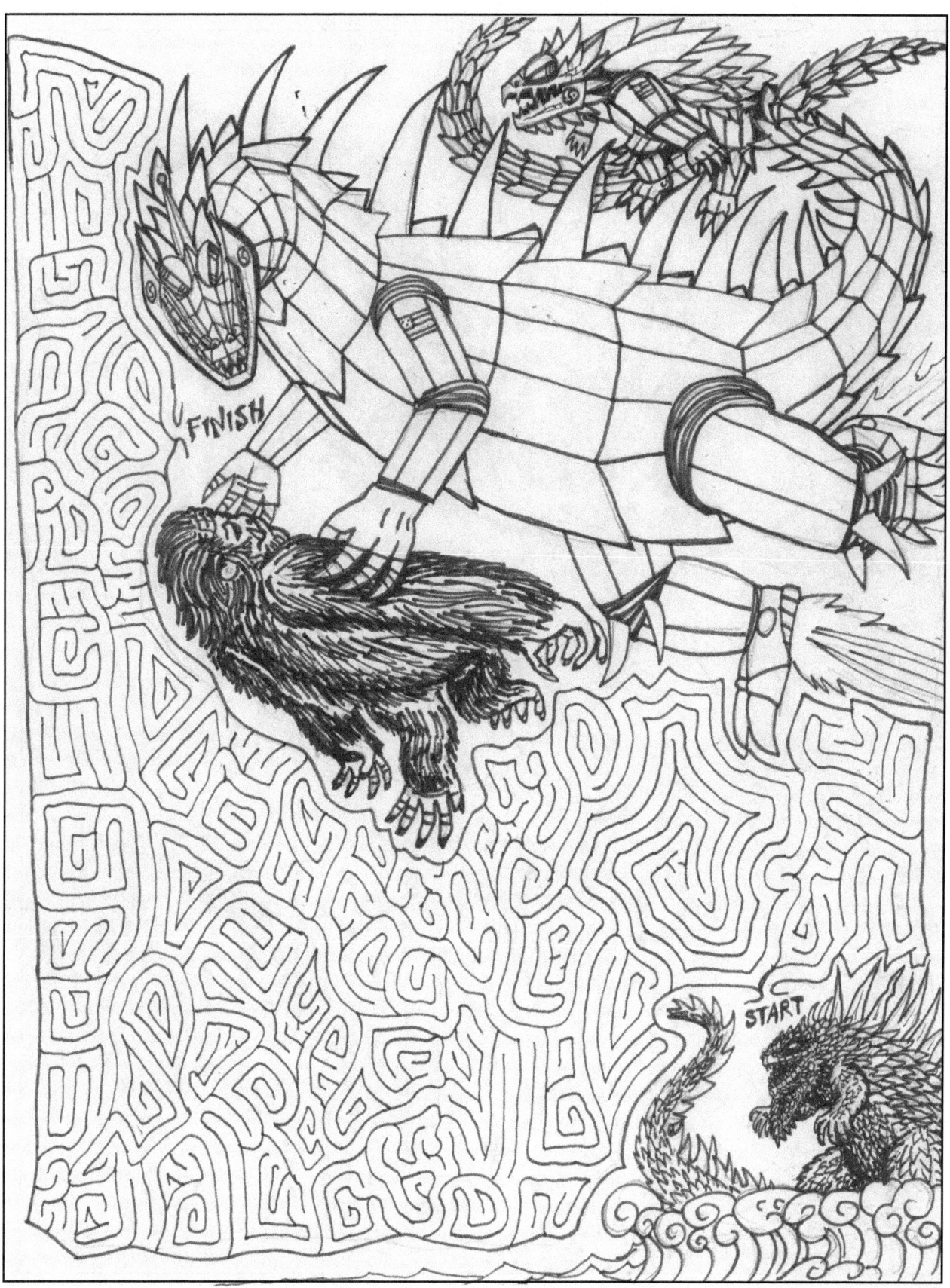

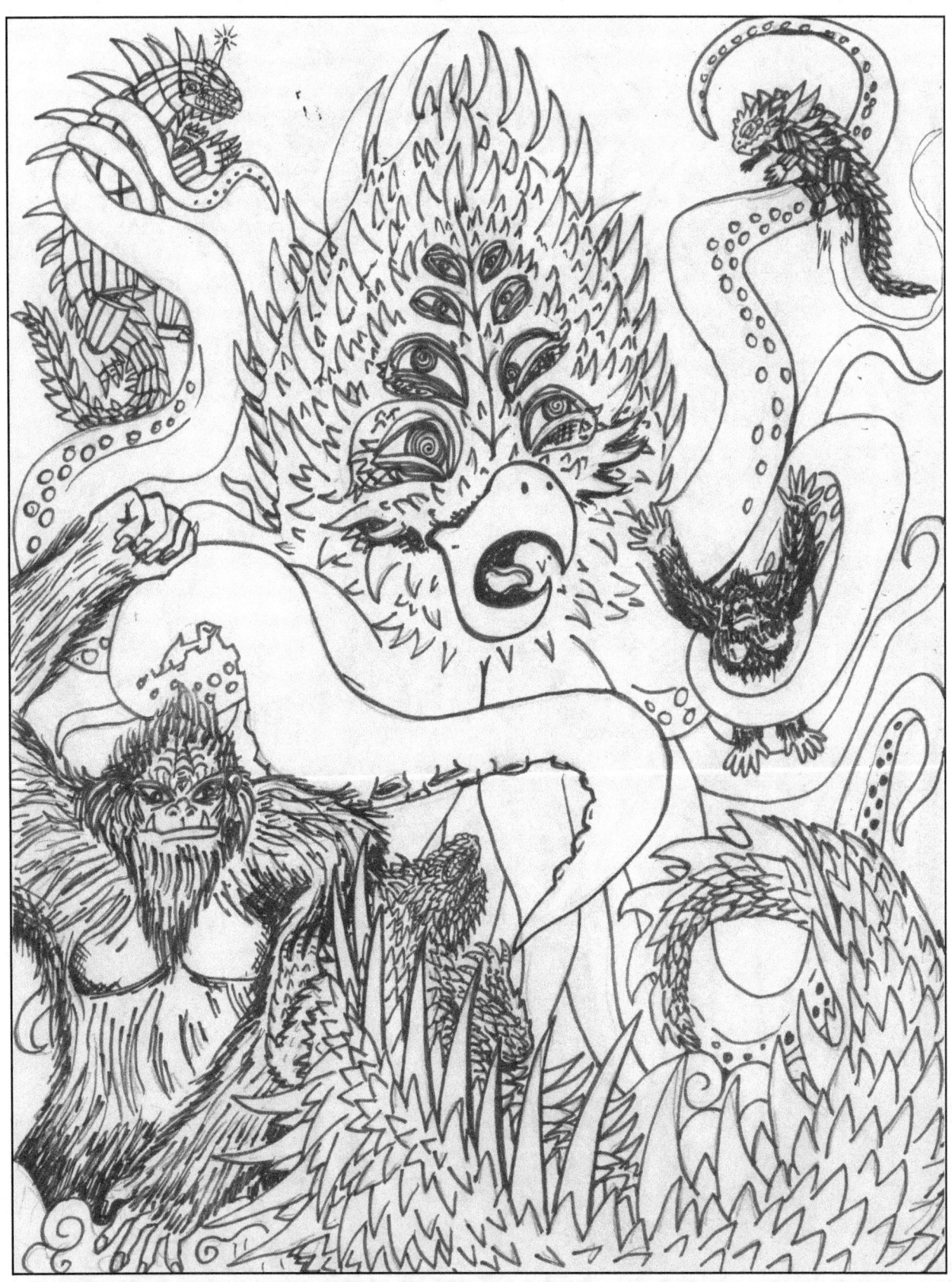

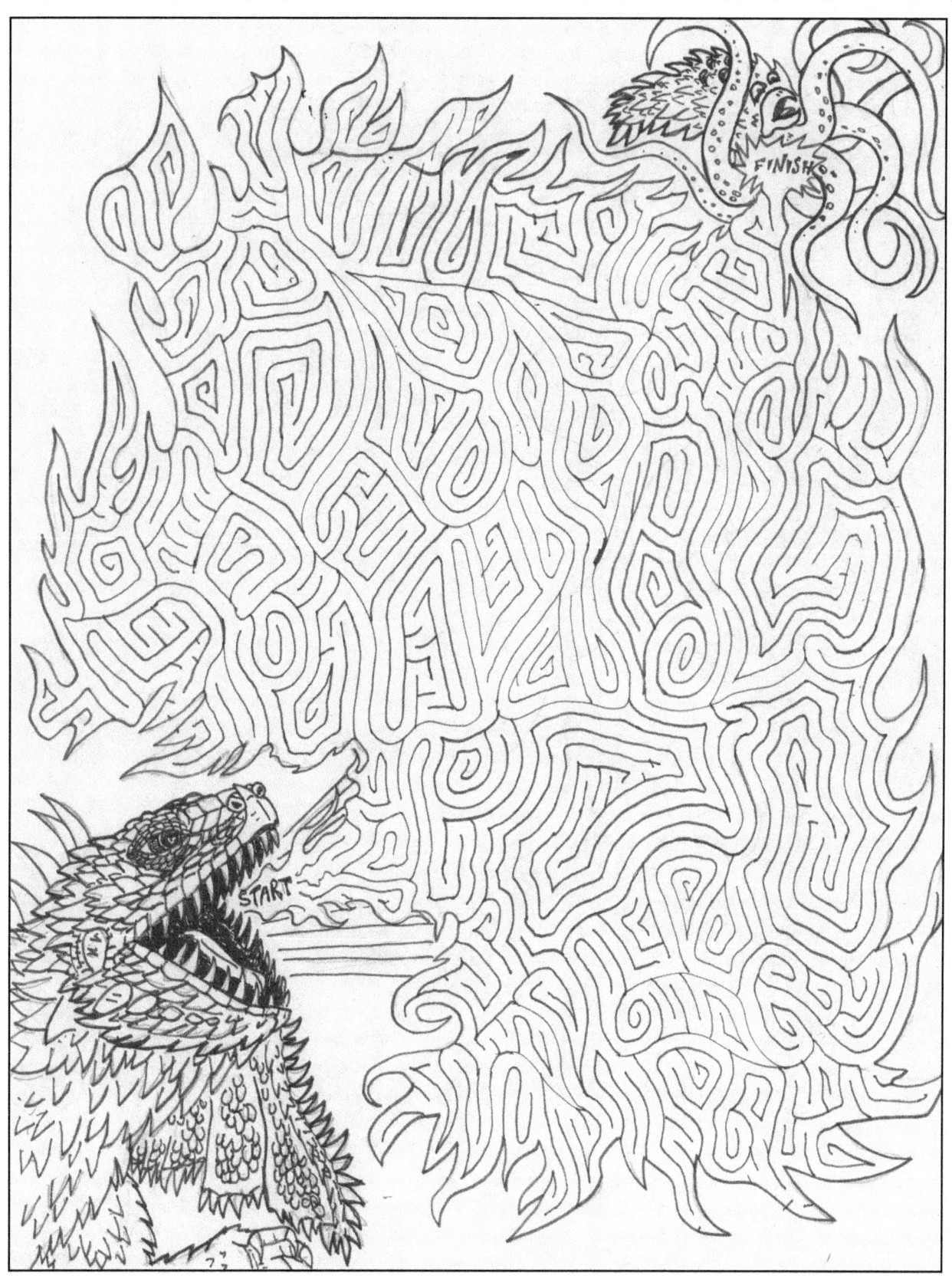

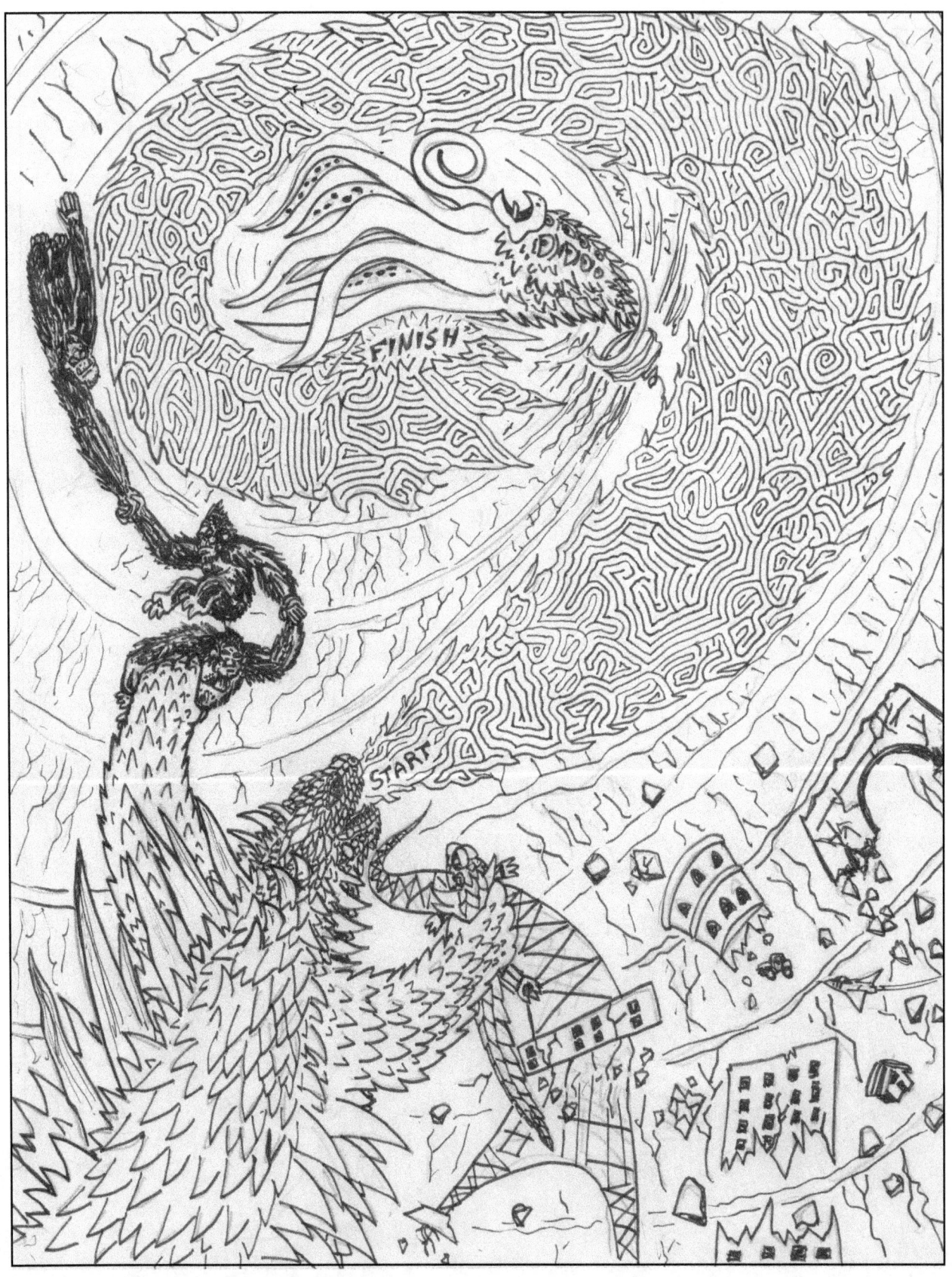

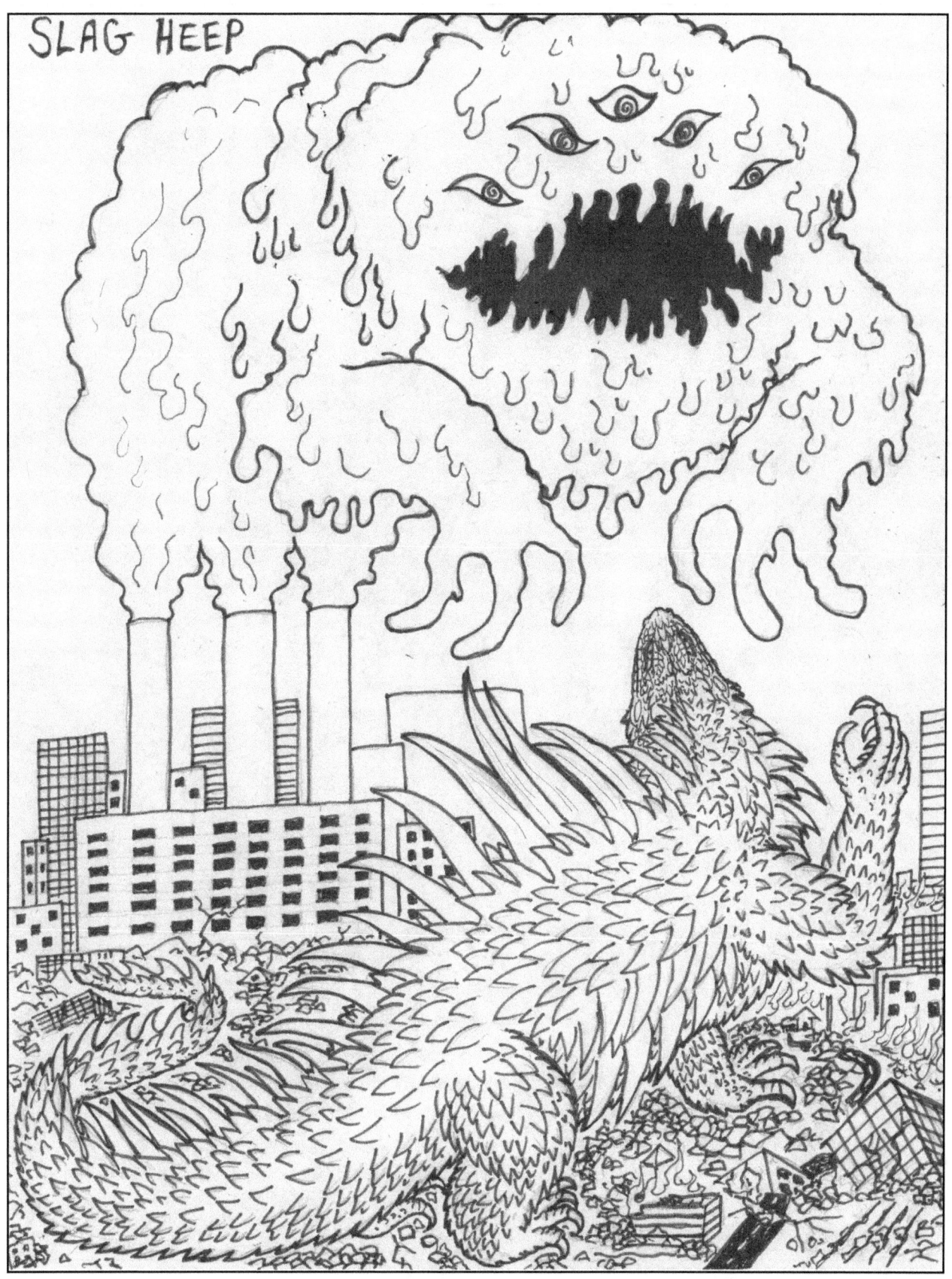

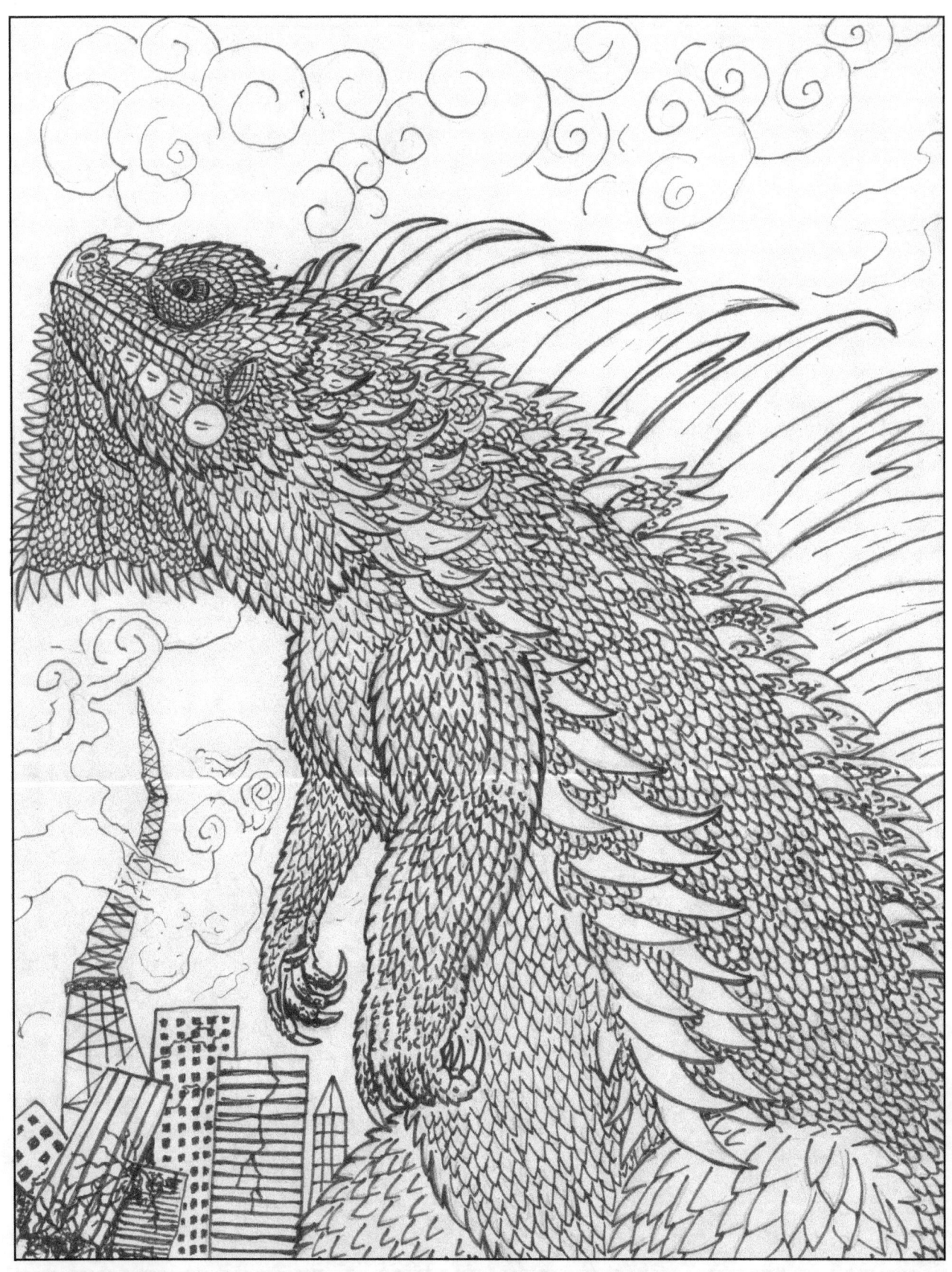

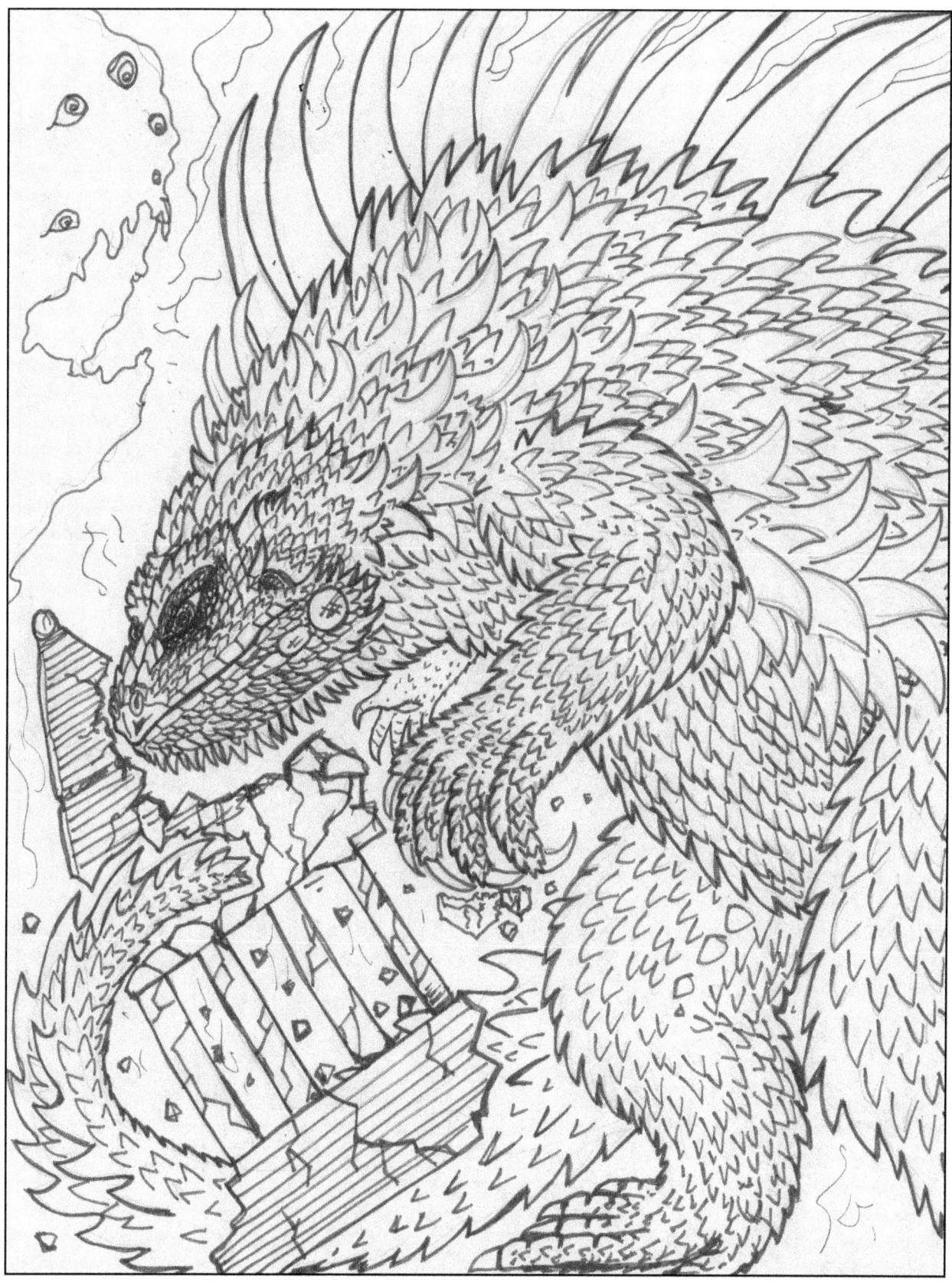

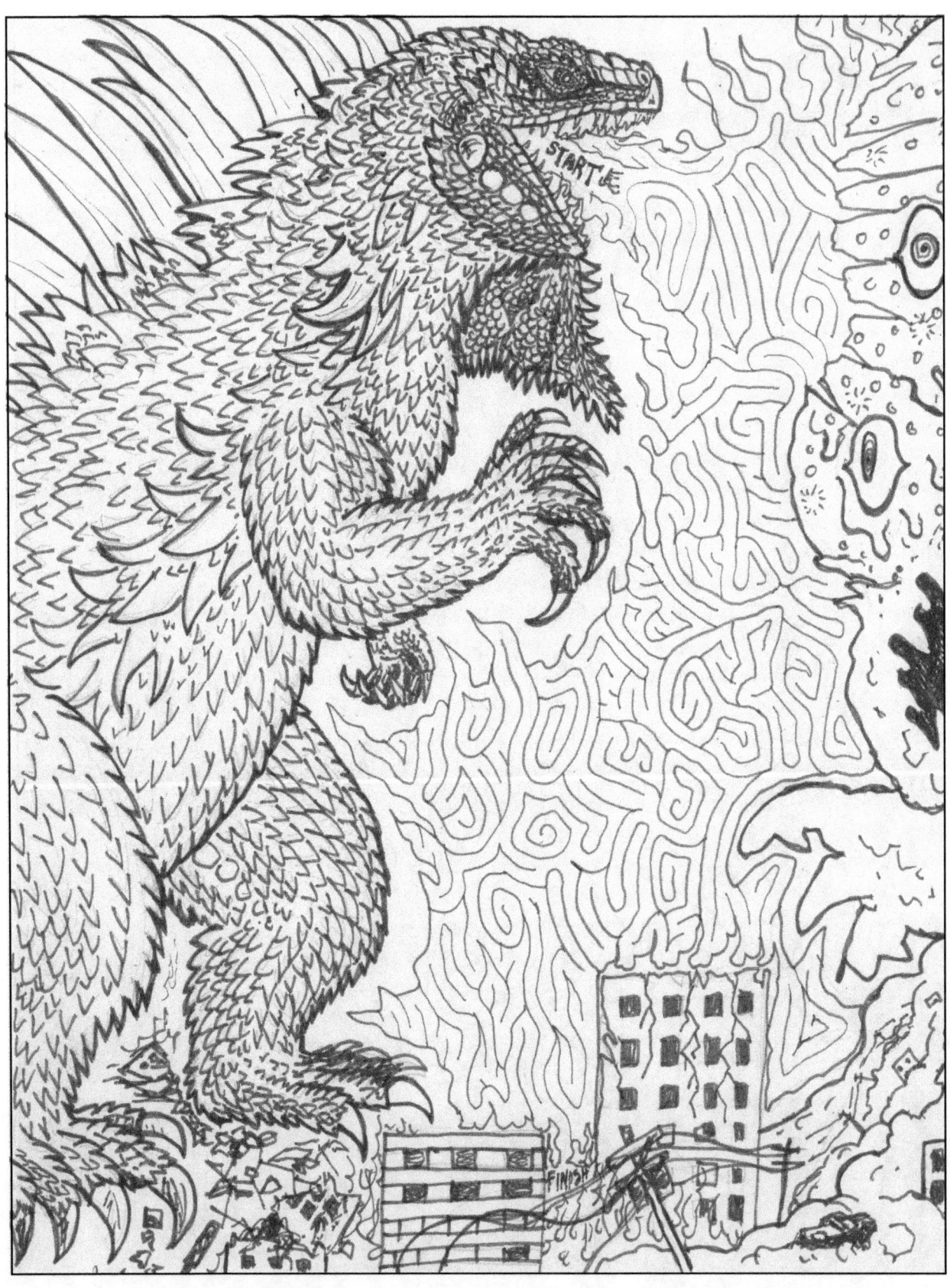

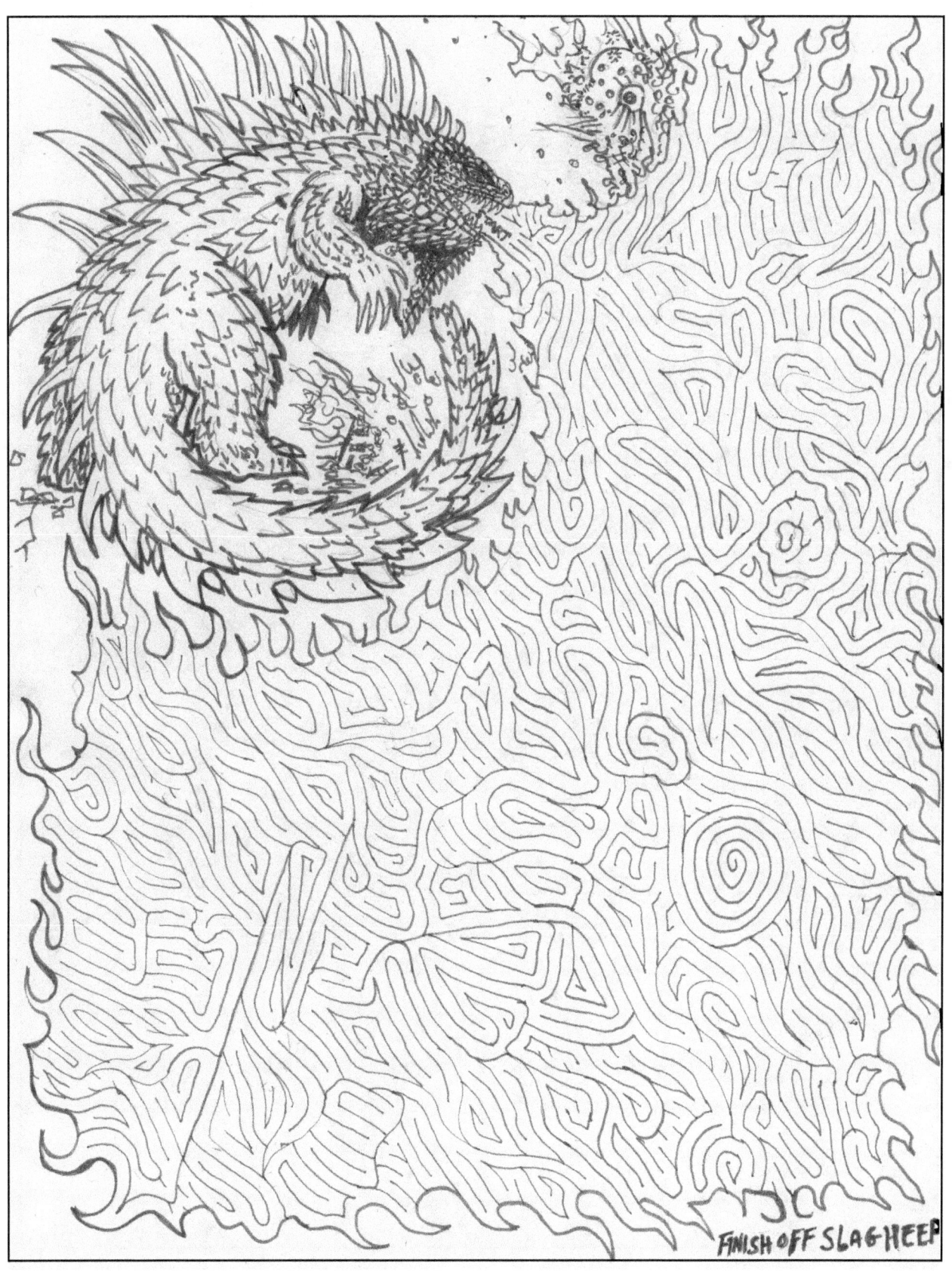

FINISH OFF SLAGHEEP

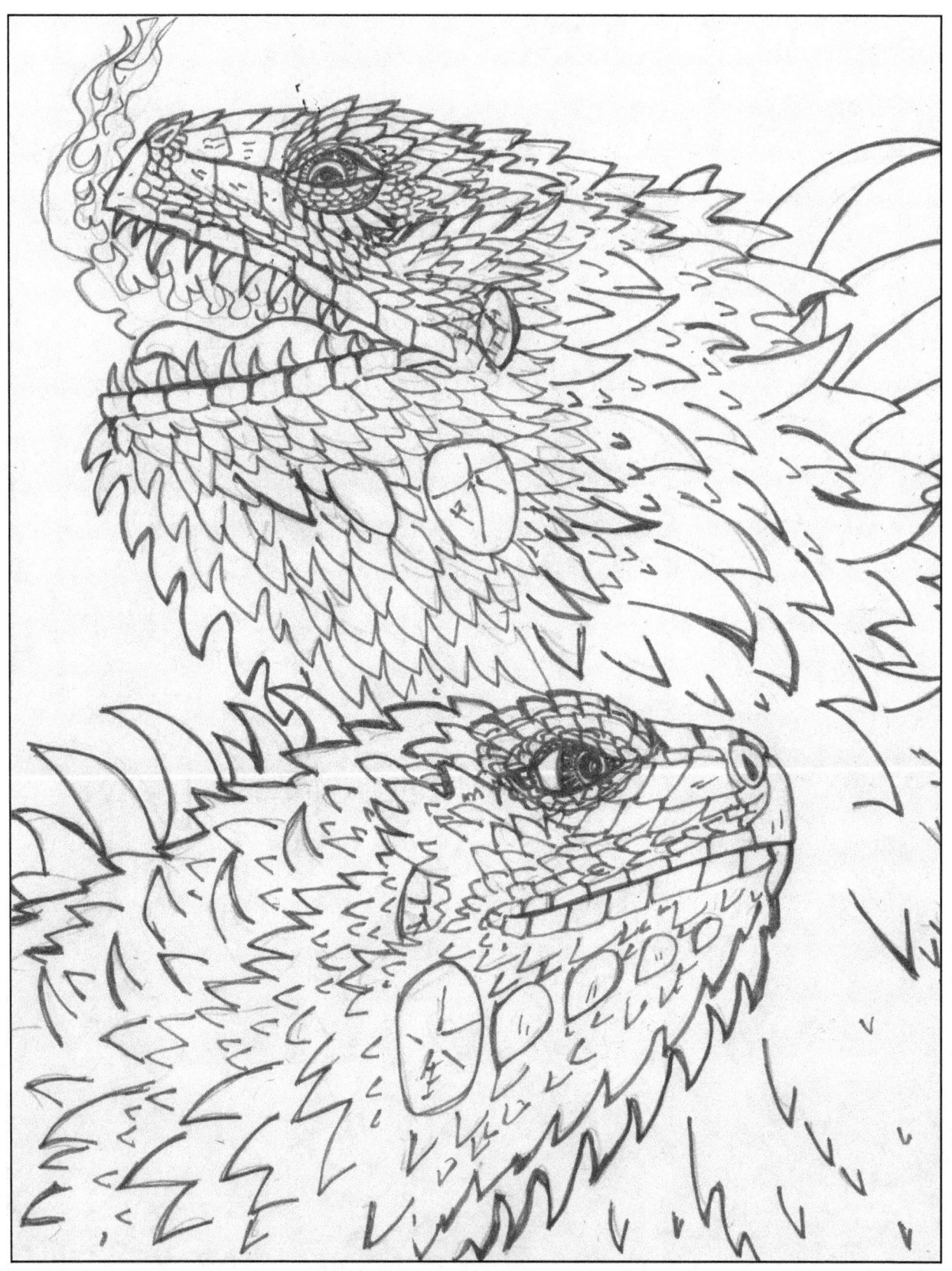

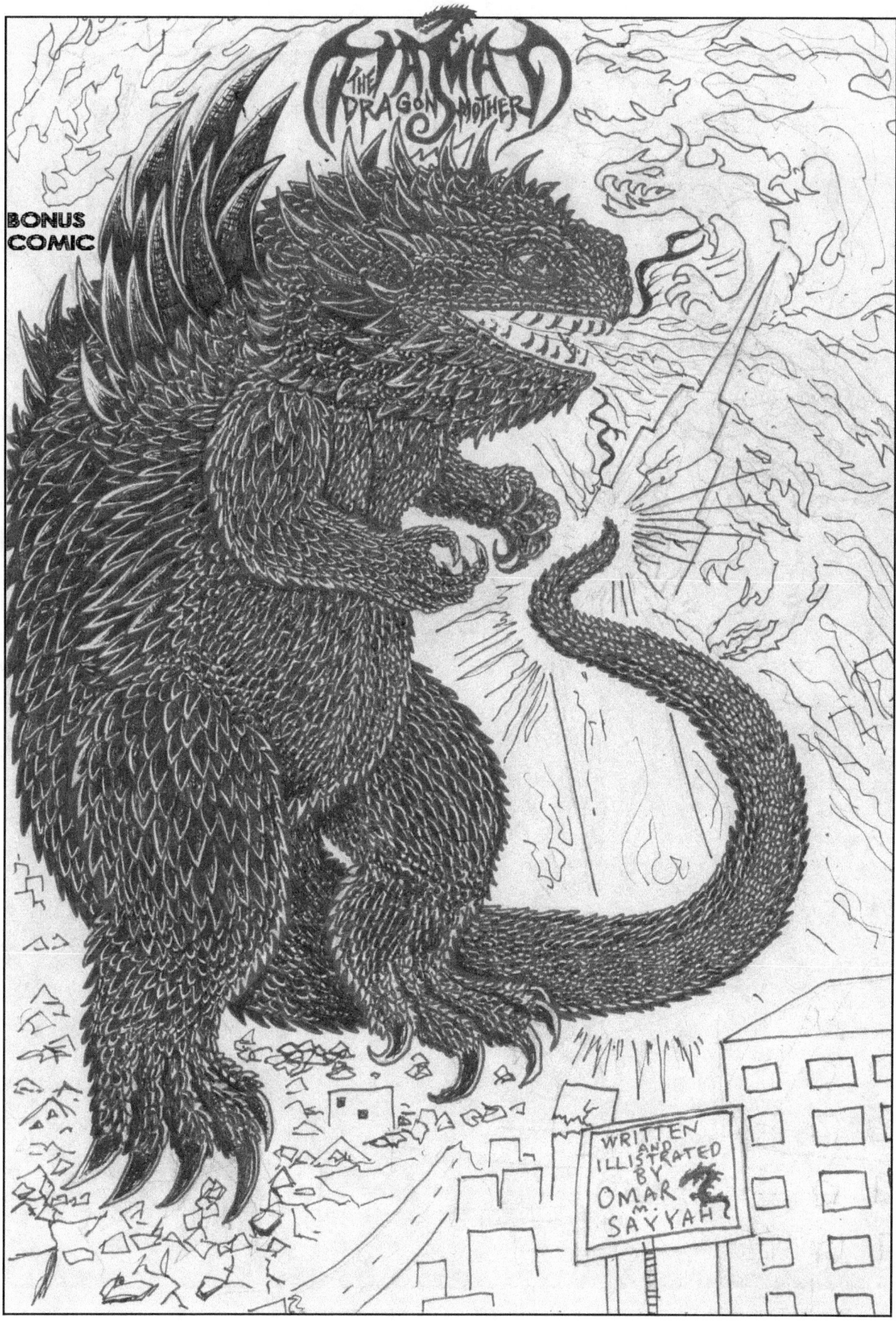

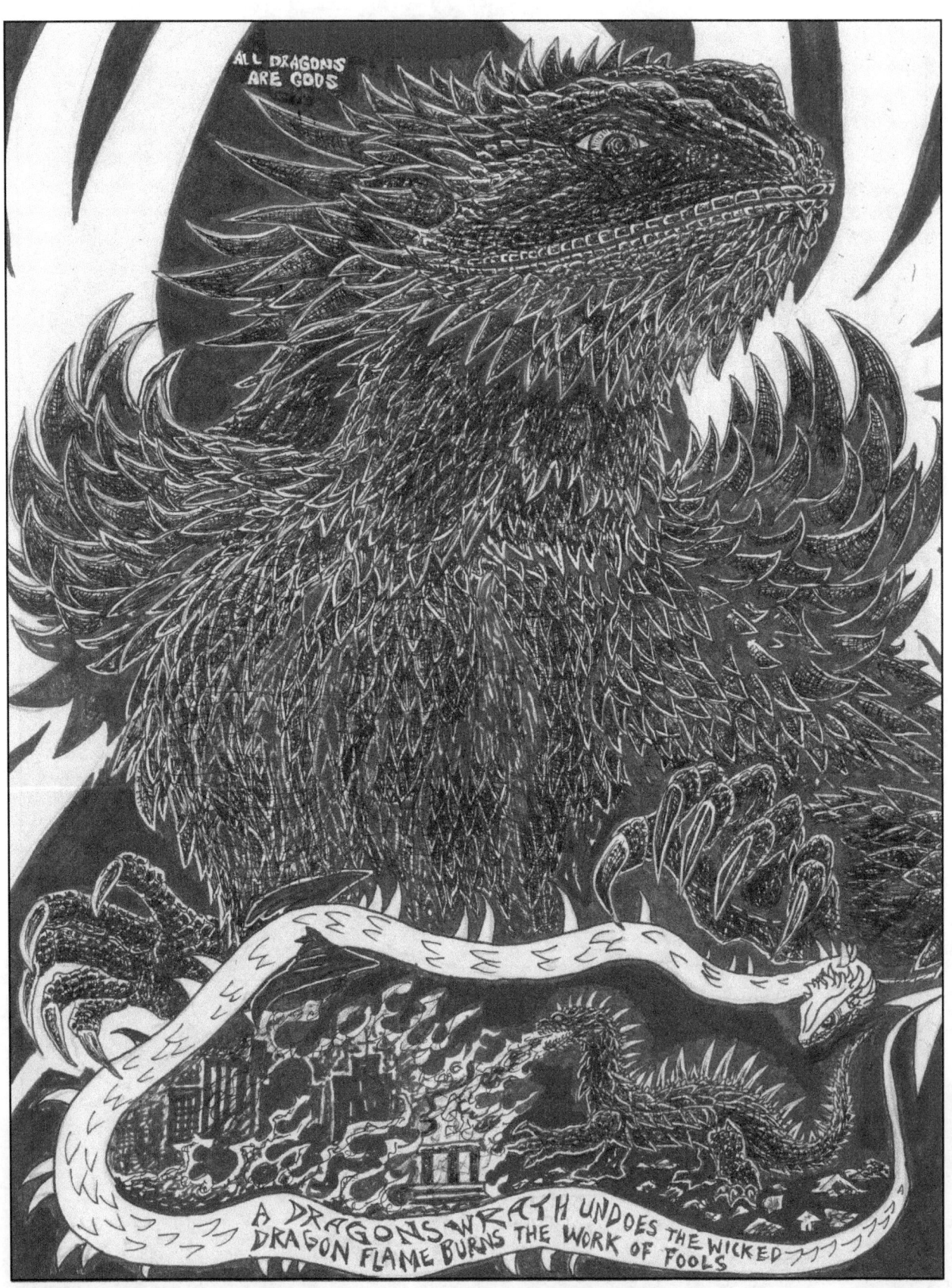

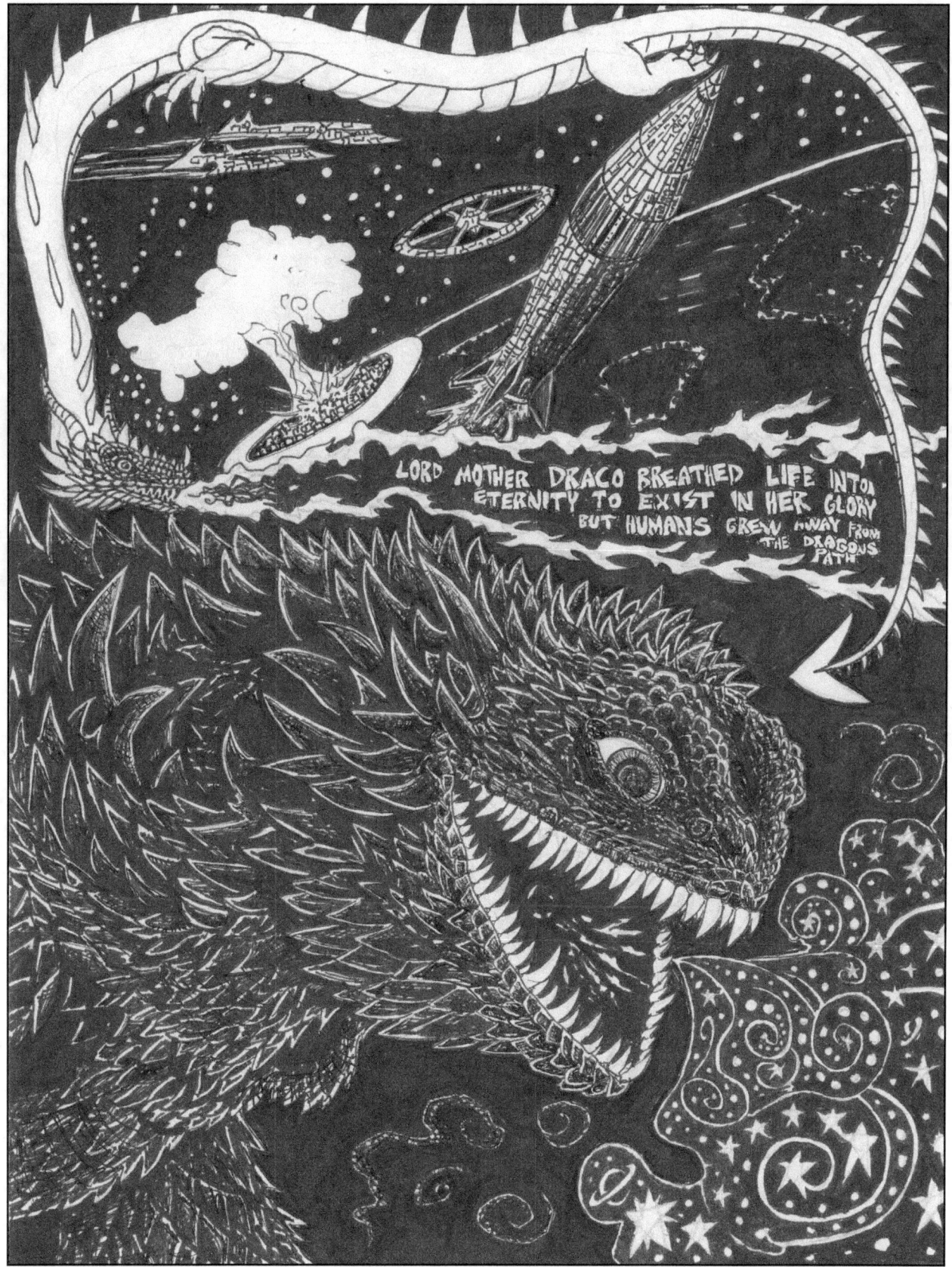

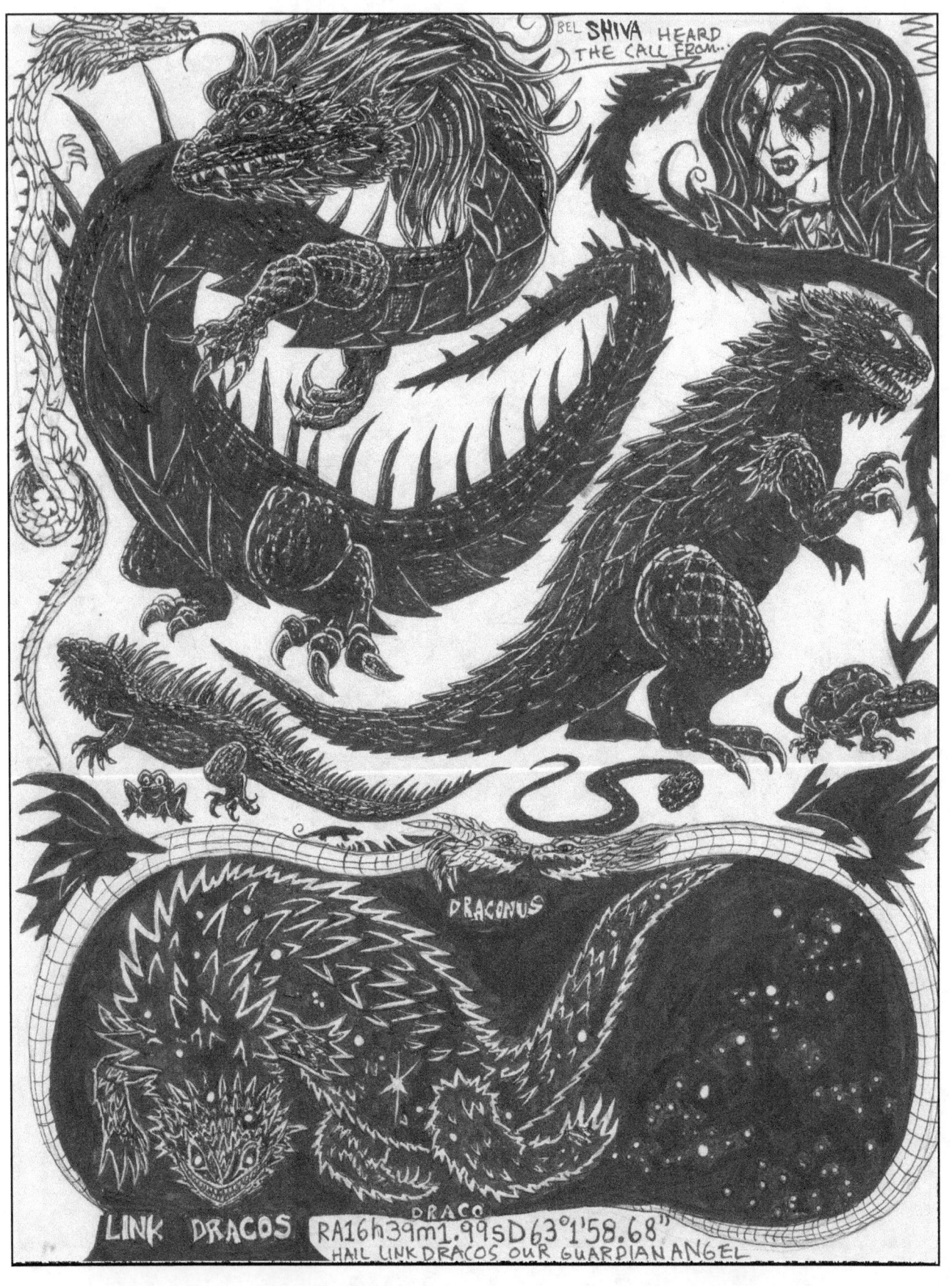

BEL **SHIVA** HEARD THE CALL FROM...

DRACONUS

LINK DRACOS

DRACO

RA16h39m1.99sD63°1'58.68"

HAIL LINK DRACOS OUR GUARDIAN ANGEL

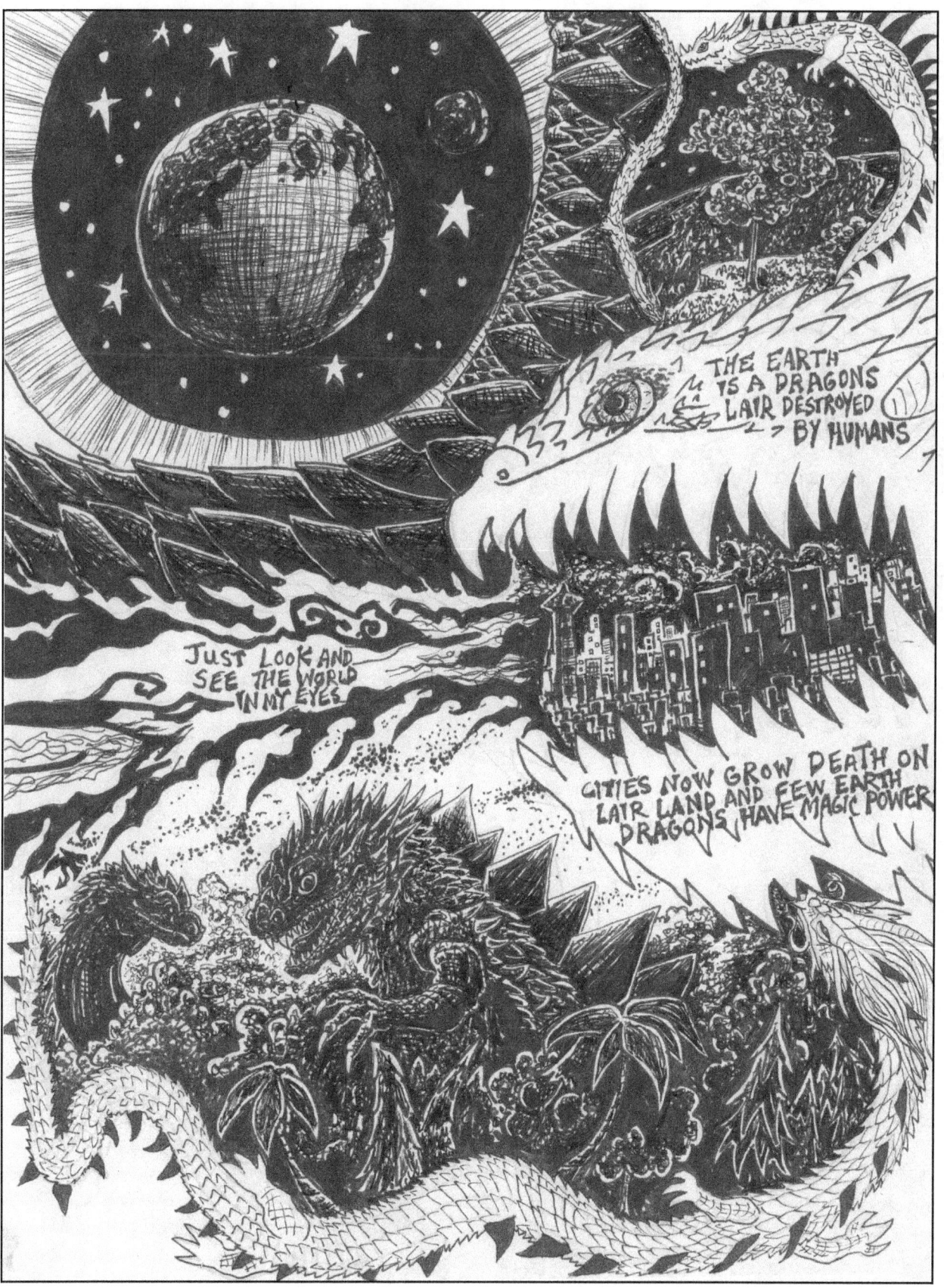

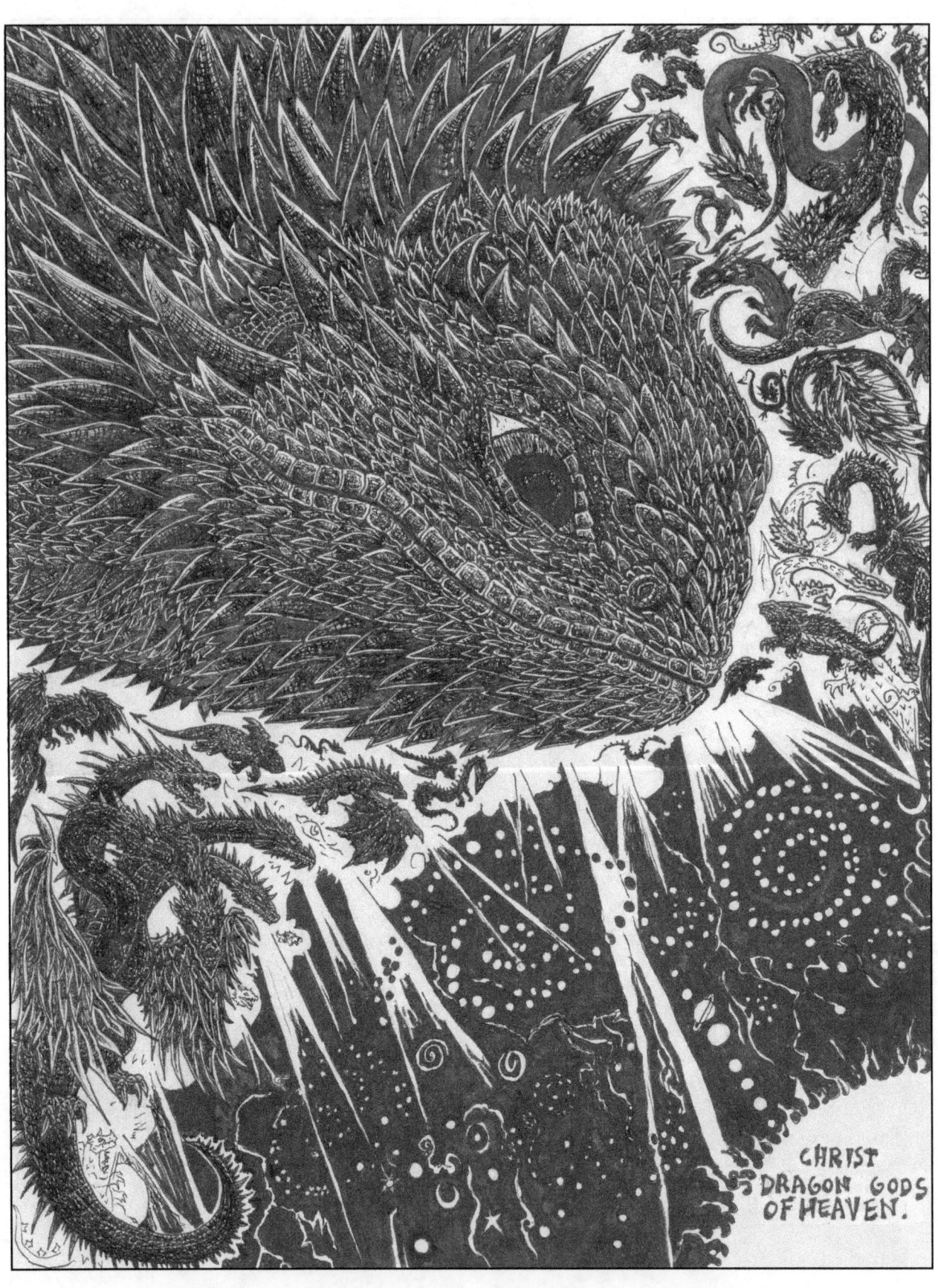

CHRIST
DRAGON GODS
OF HEAVEN.

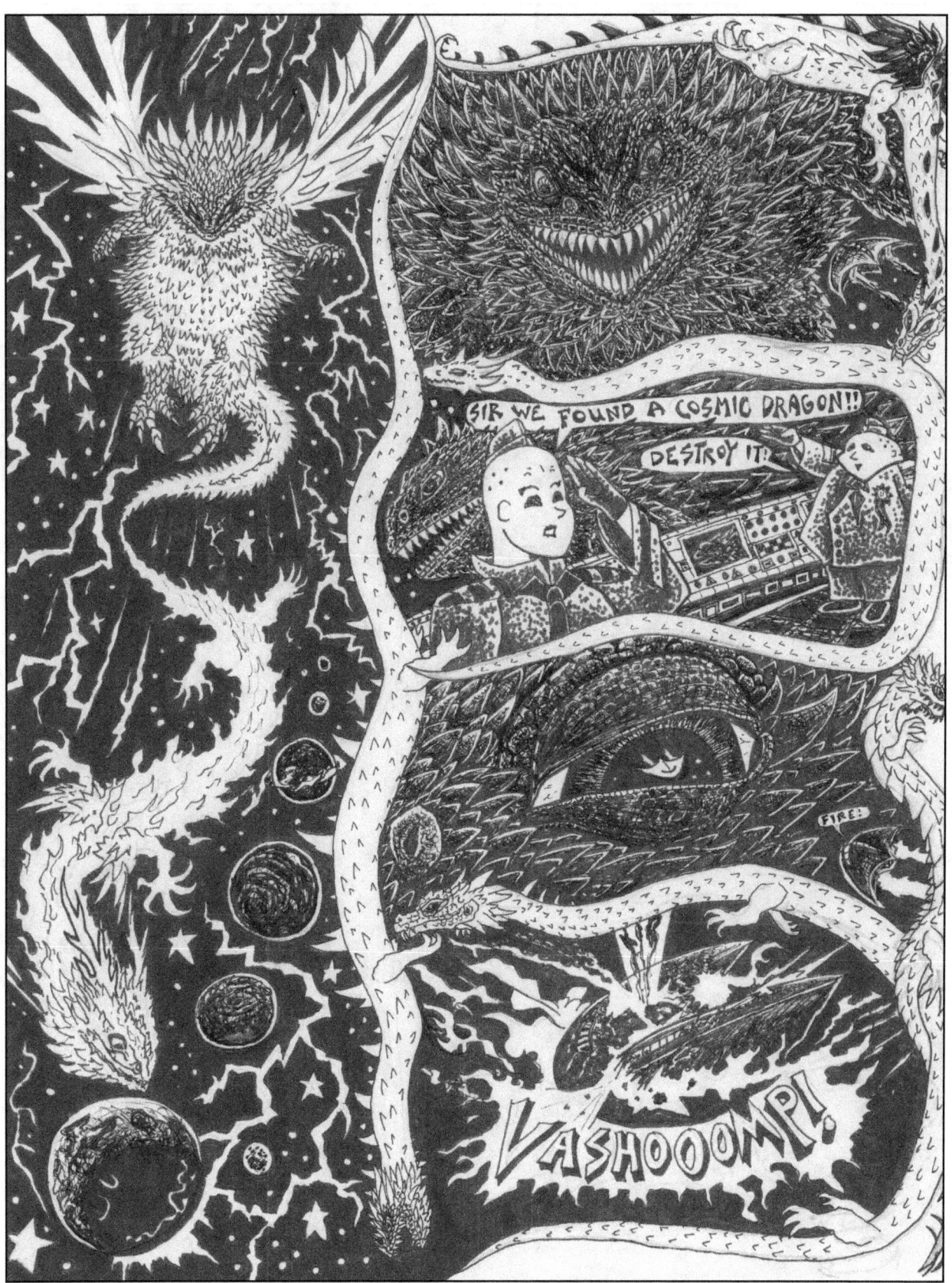

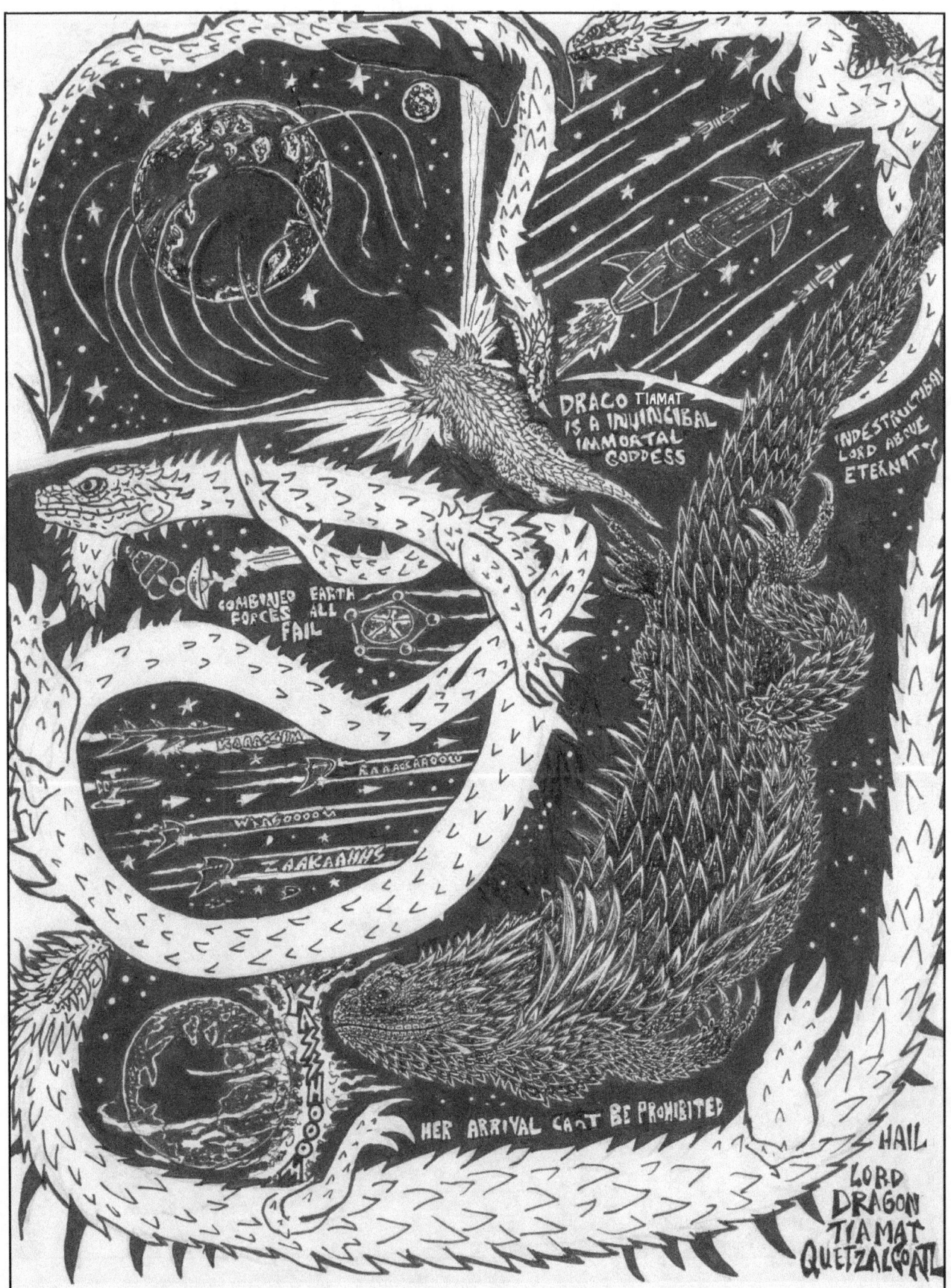

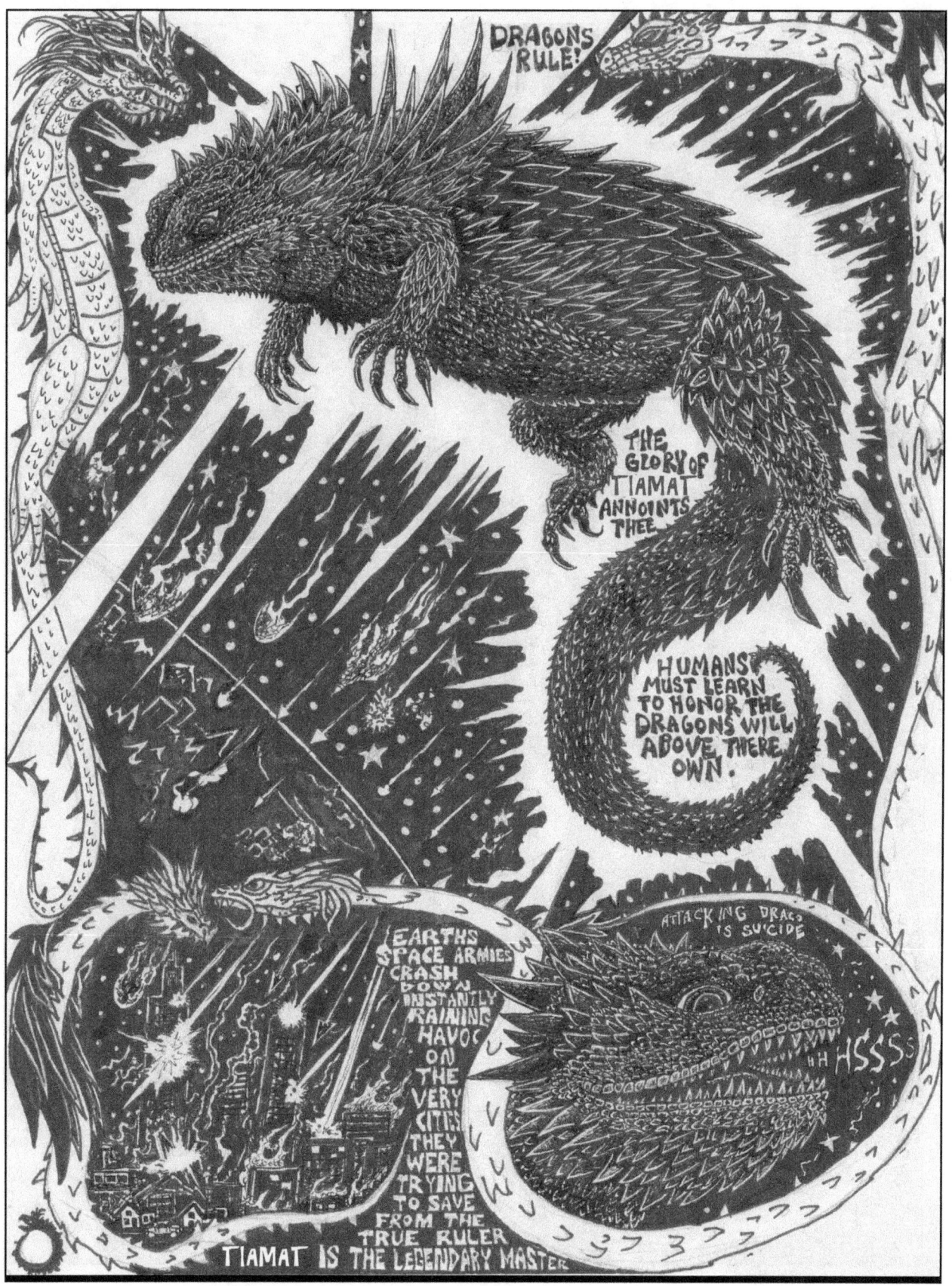

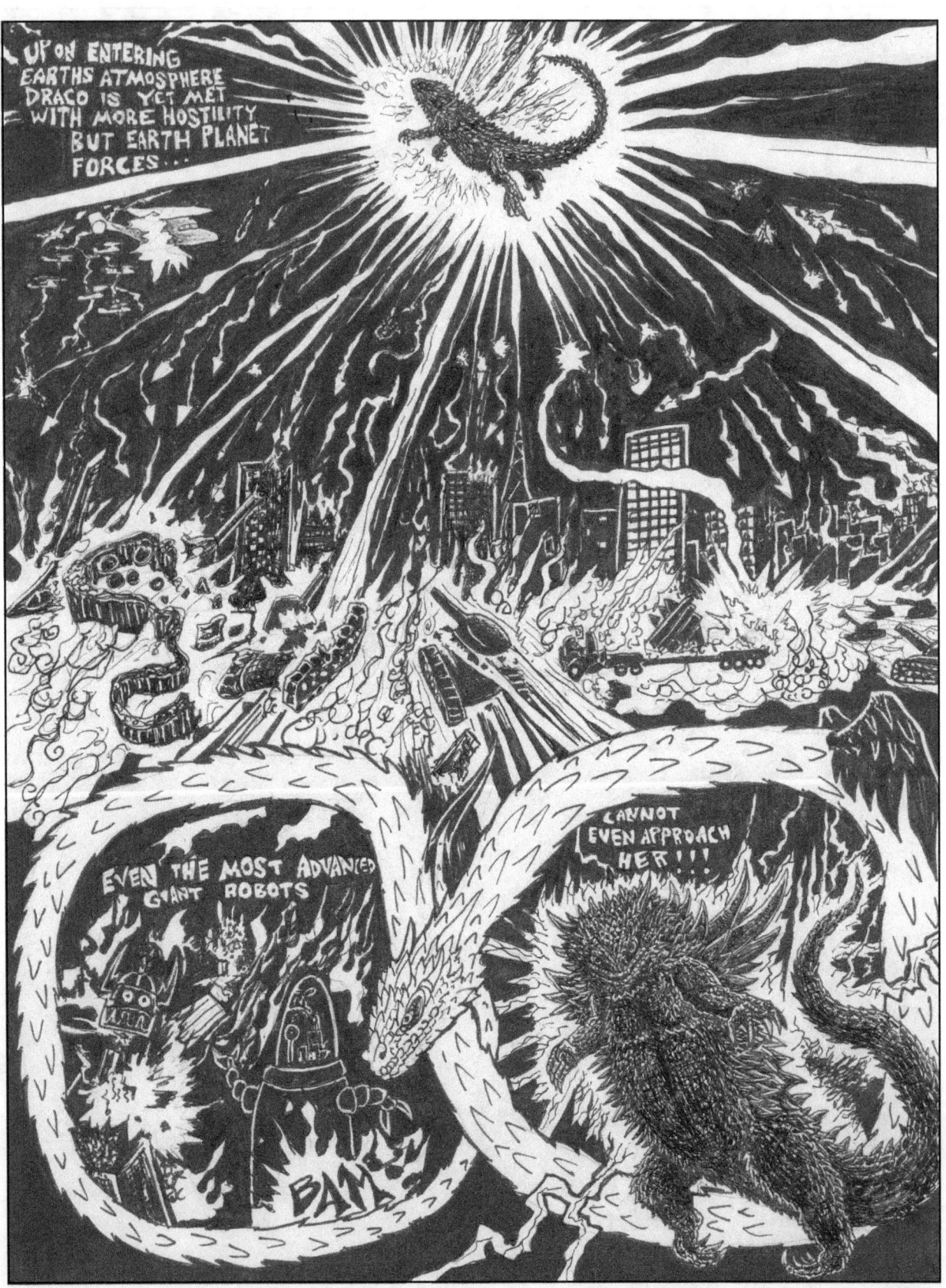

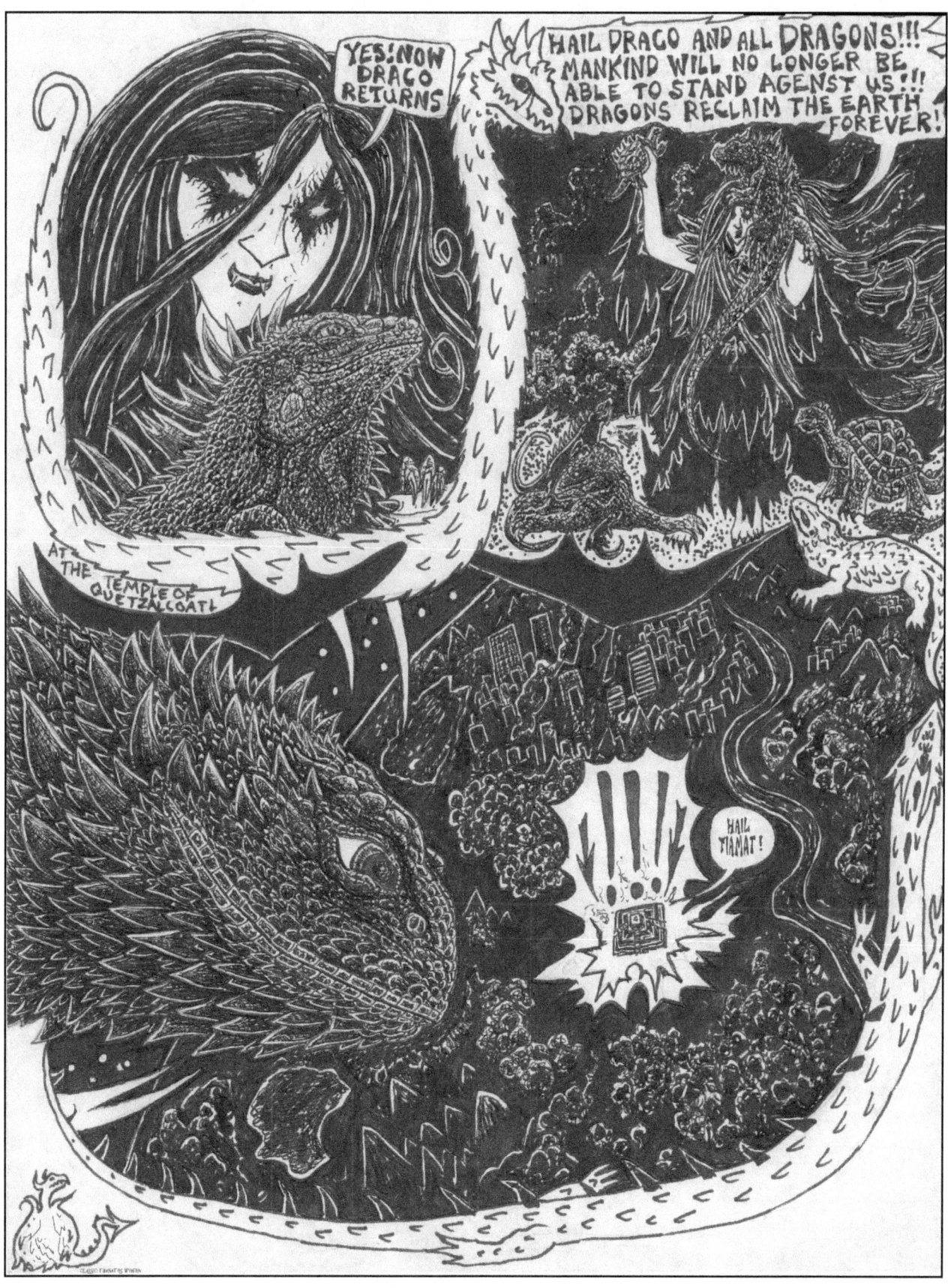

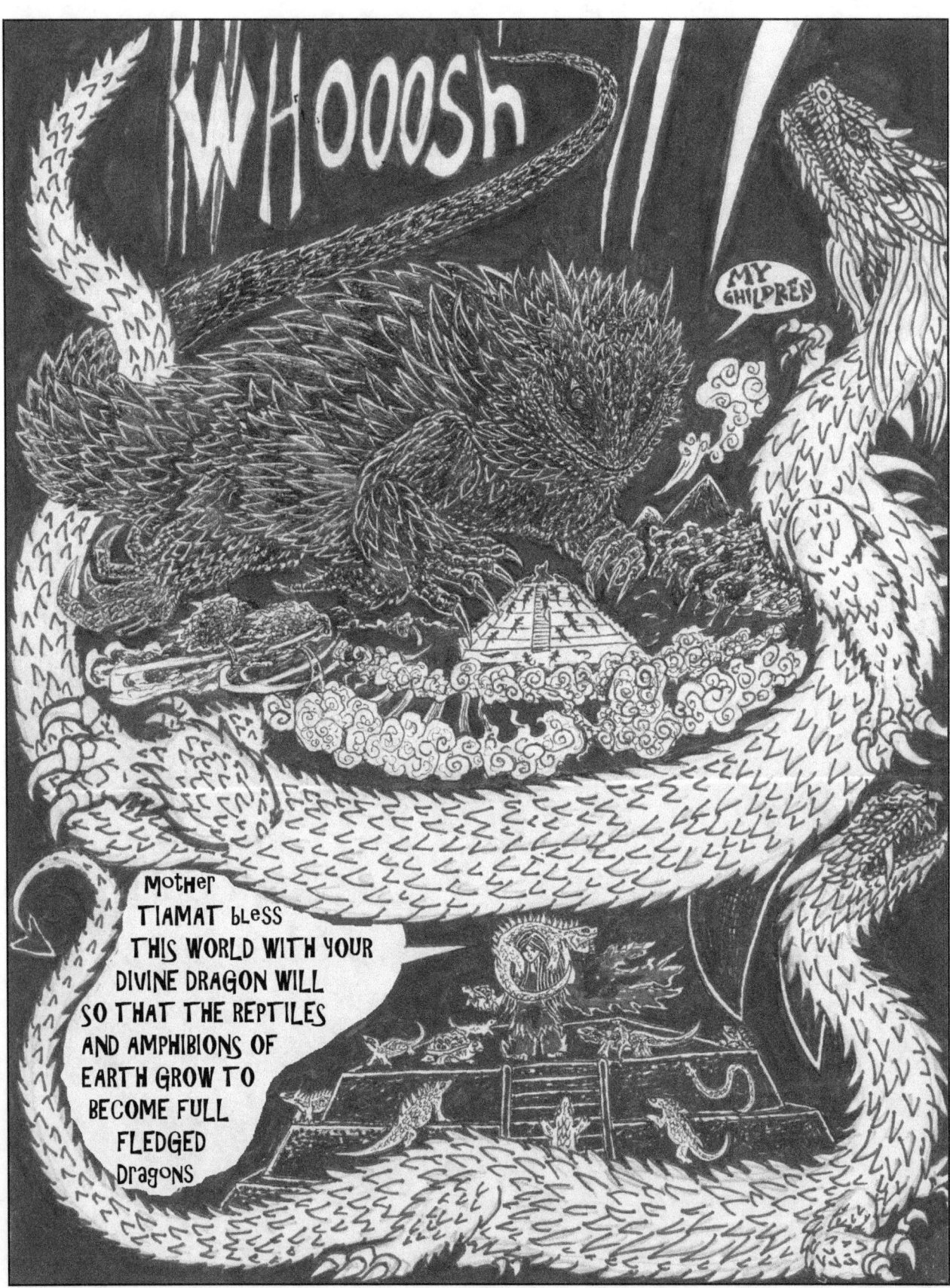

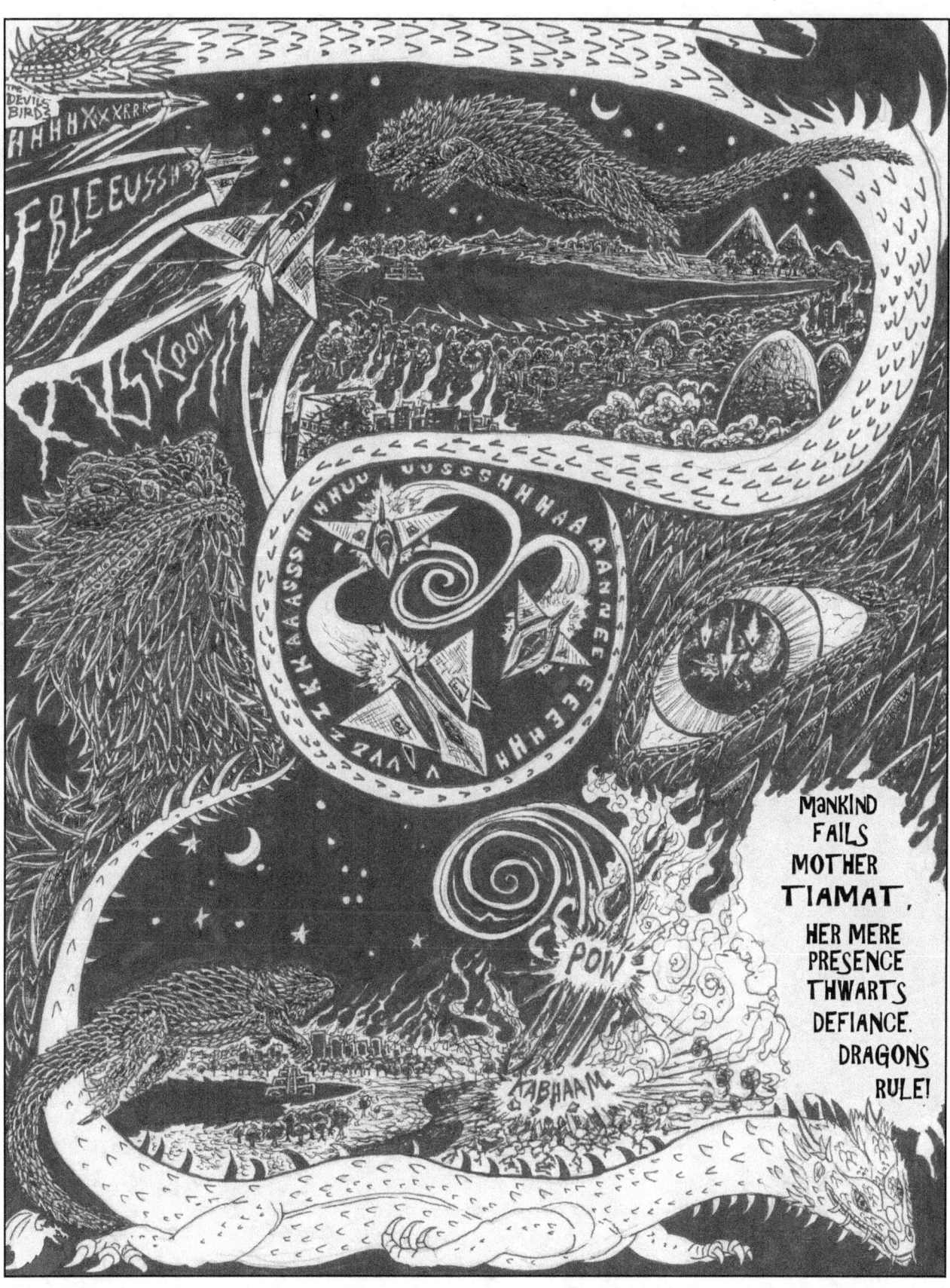

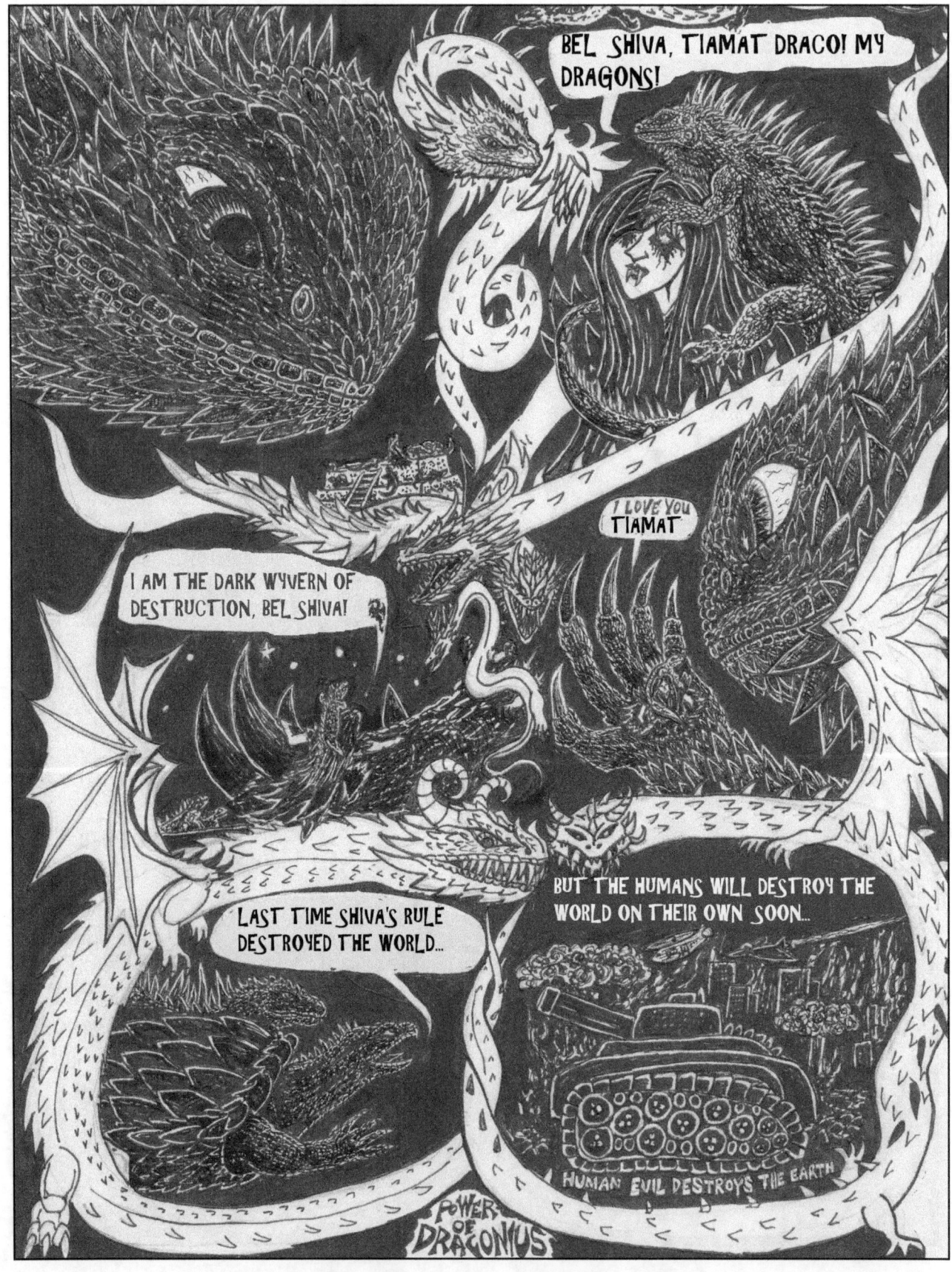

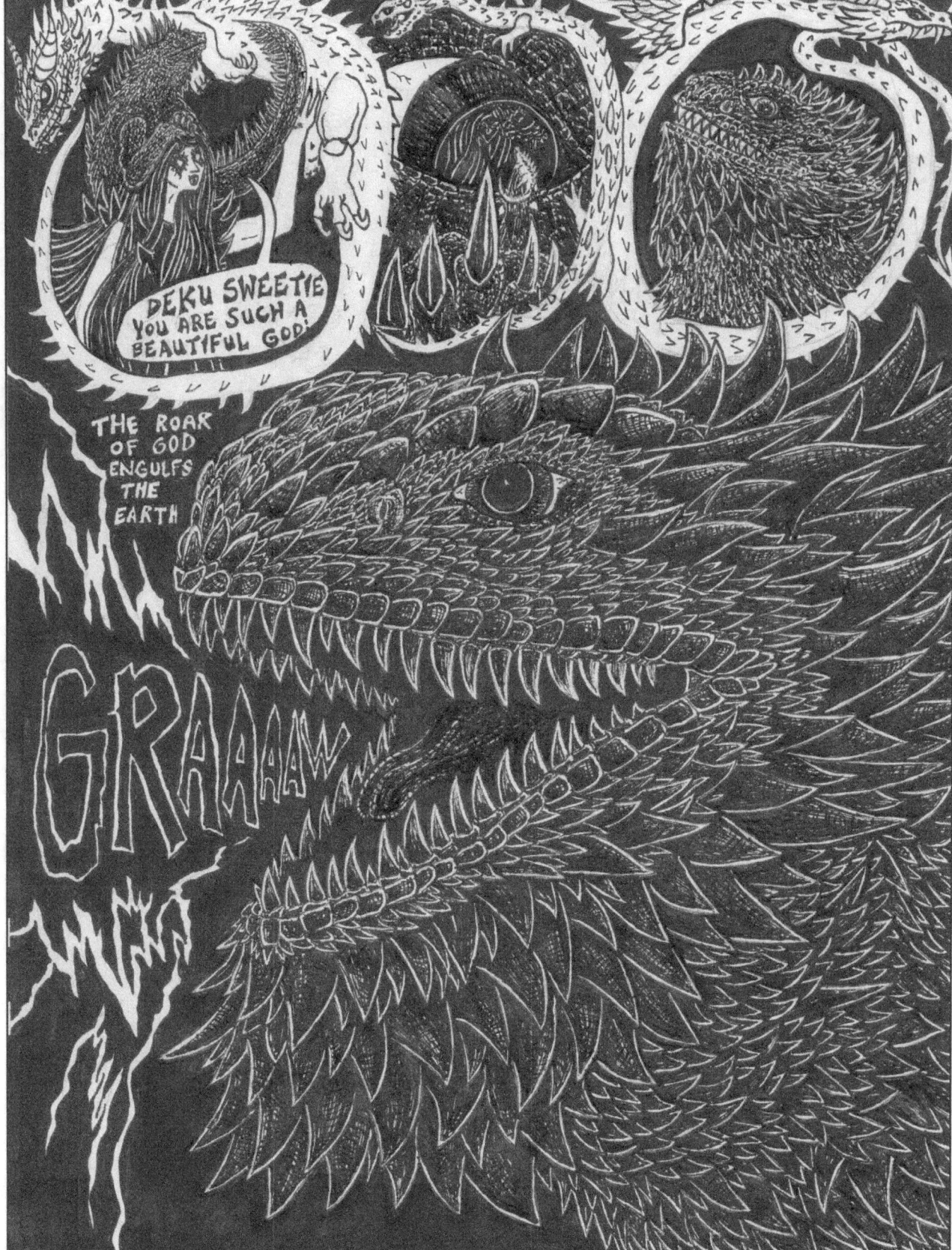

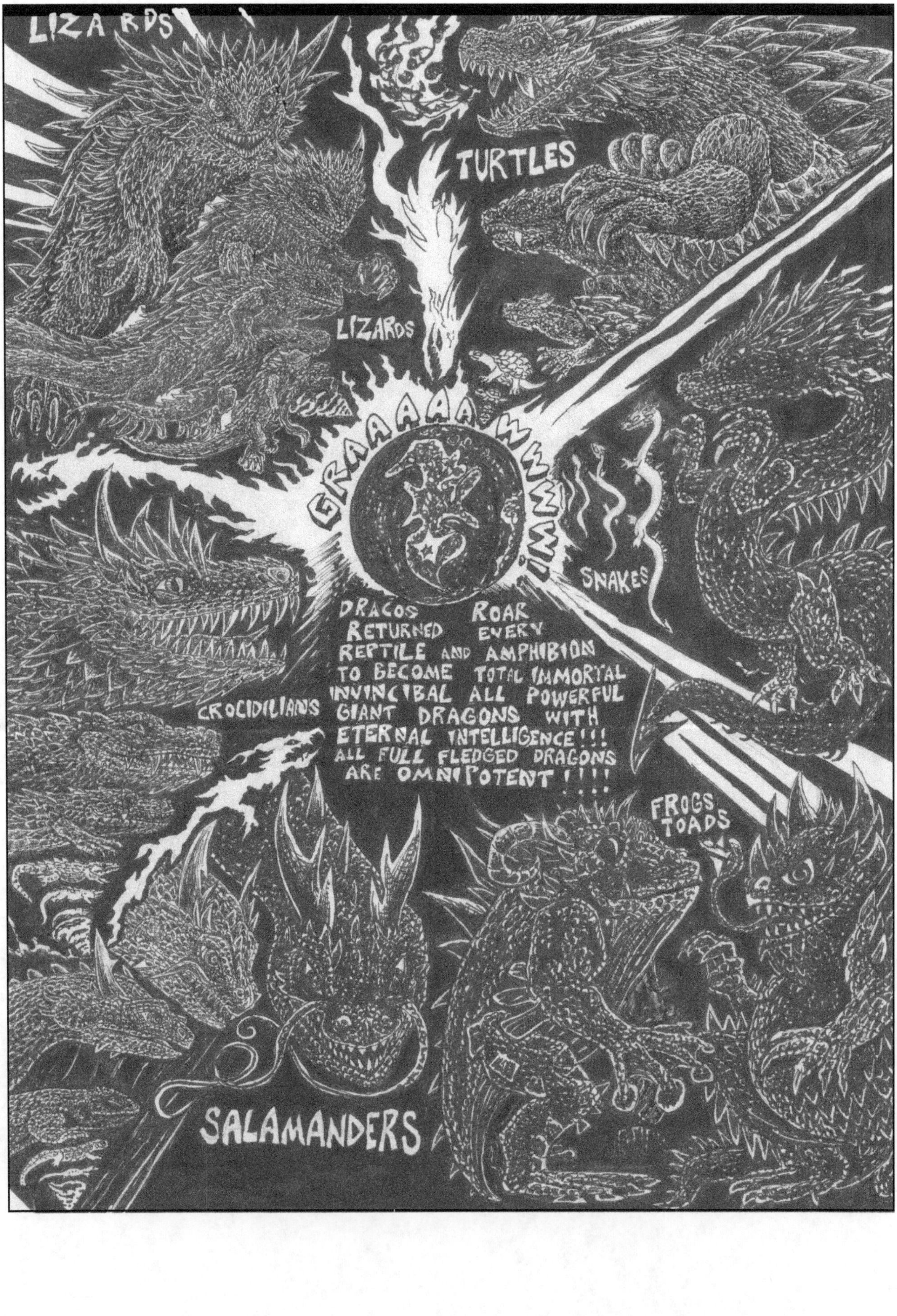

LIZARDS

TURTLES

LIZARDS

GRAAAAAWWWW!

SNAKES

DRACOS ROAR
RETURNED EVERY
REPTILE AND AMPHIBION
TO BECOME TOTAL IMMORTAL
INVINCIBAL ALL POWERFUL
GIANT DRAGONS WITH
ETERNAL INTELLIGENCE!!!
ALL FULL FLEDGED DRAGONS
ARE OMNIPOTENT!!!!

CROCIDILIANS

FROGS
TOADS

SALAMANDERS

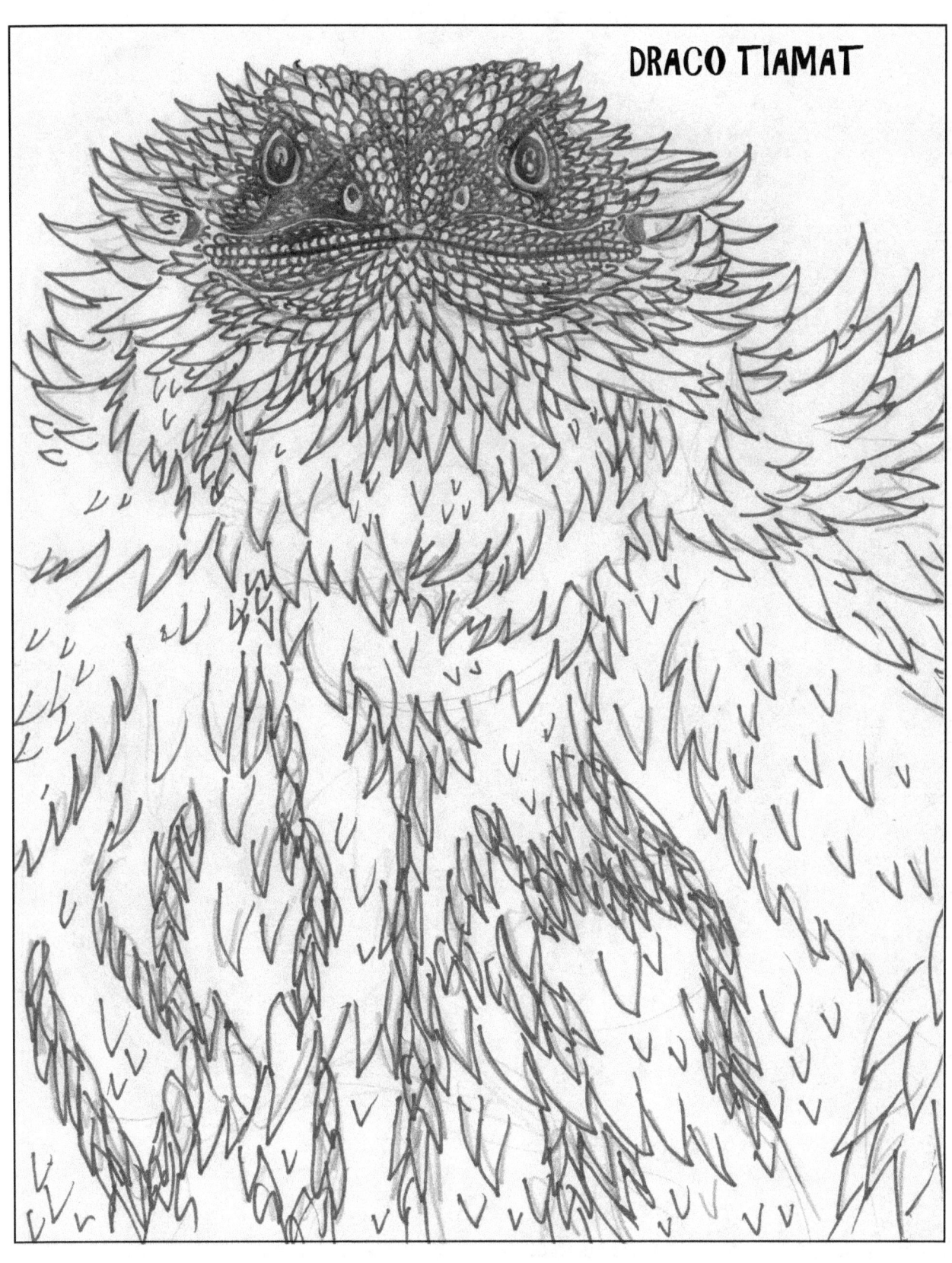

DRACO TIAMAT

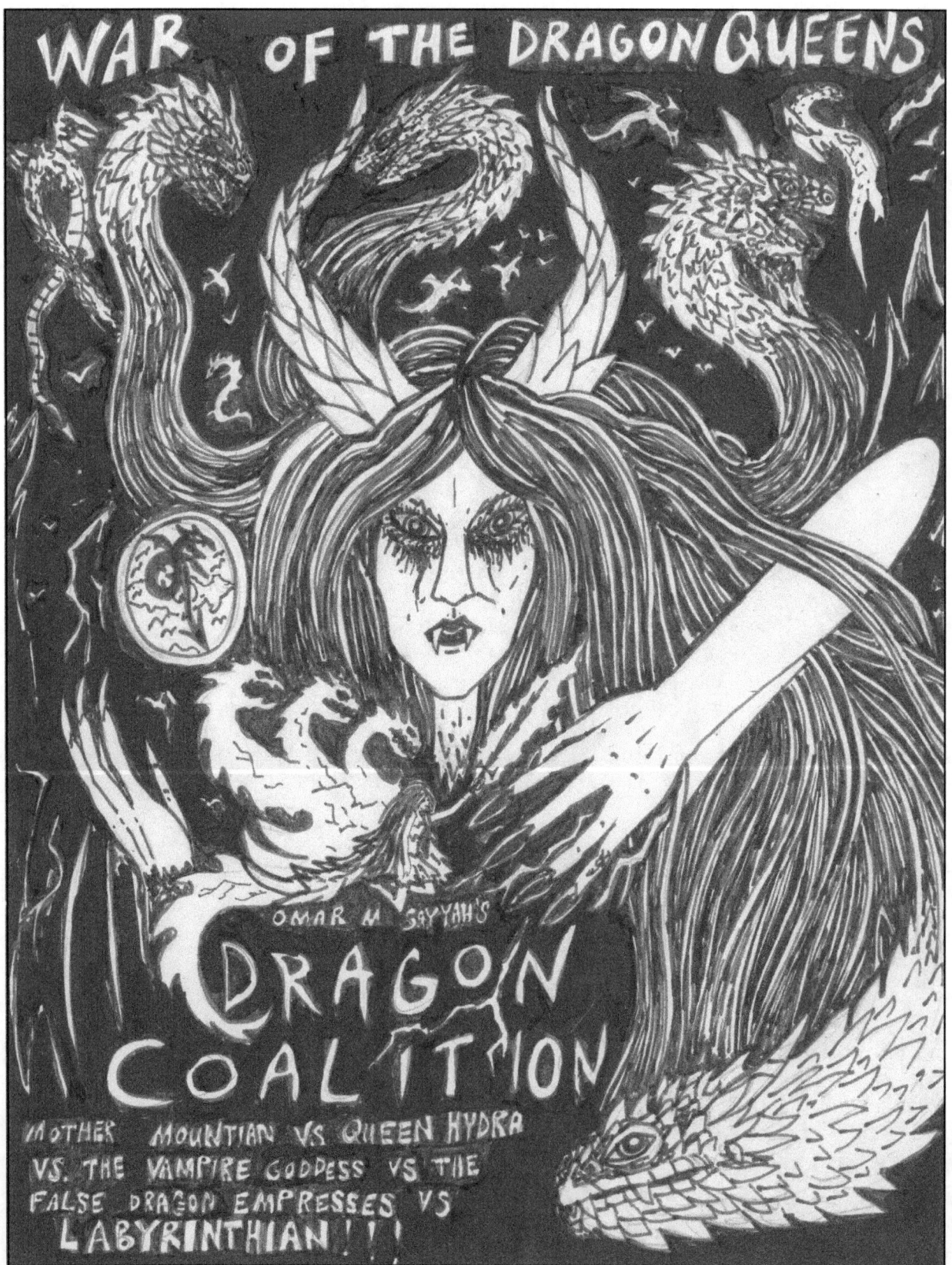

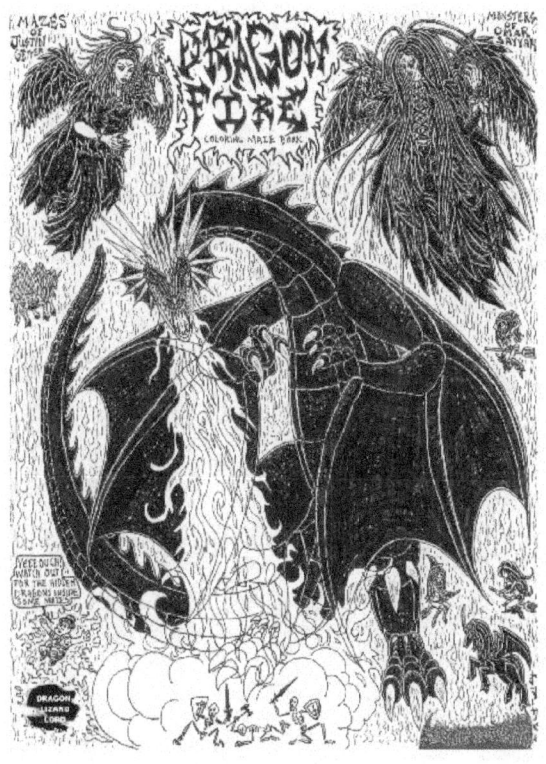

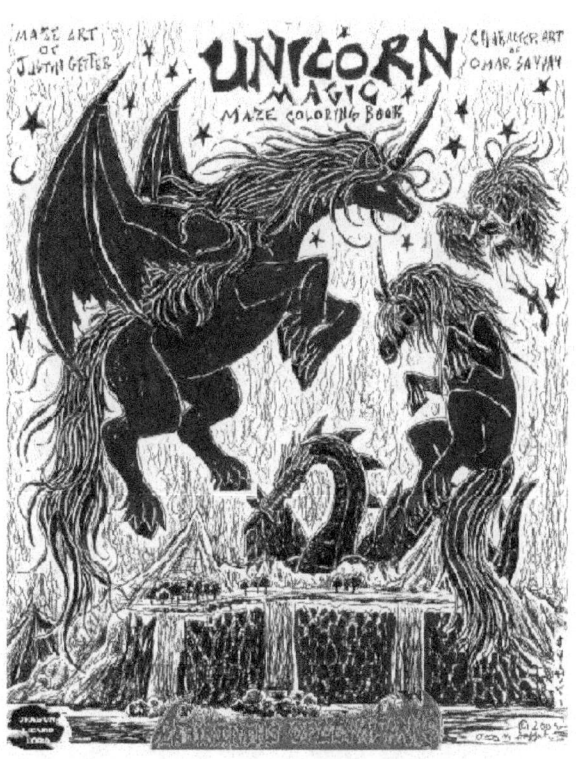

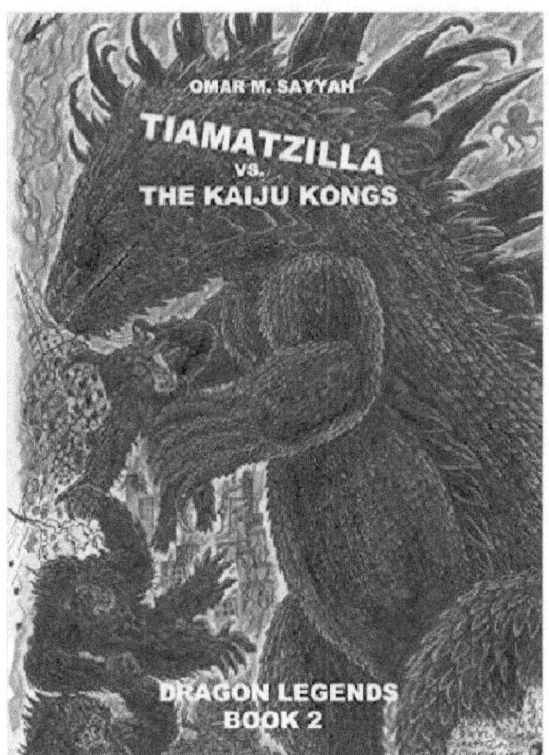

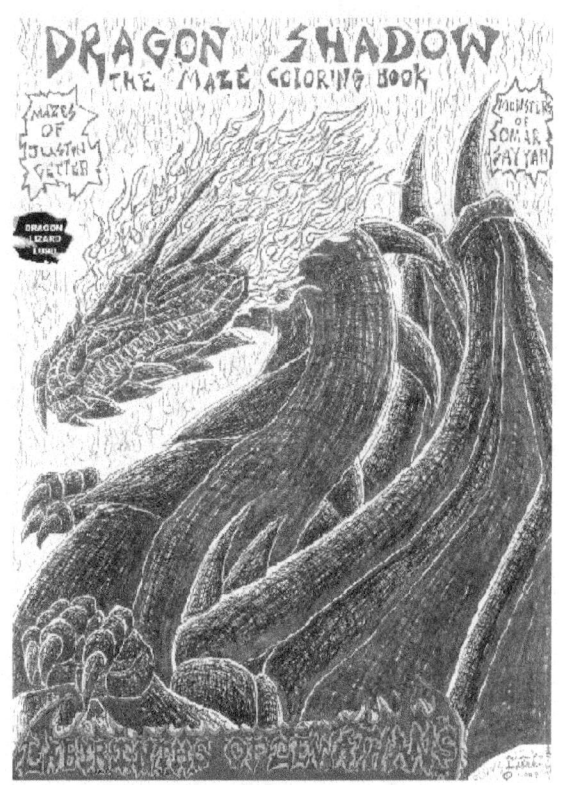

LOOK FOR THESE OTHER AMAZING BOOKS FROM
DRAGON LIZARD LORD
CONTACT DRAGONLIZARDLORD@GMAIL.COM